SCRIPTURE UNION

BIBLE
STUDY
BOOKS

1 and 2 Timothy, Titus, Philemon, Hebrews, James

LEON MORRIS, M.Sc., M.Th., Ph.D.

D0185205

SCRIPTURE UNION
5 WIGMORE STREET
LONDON, W1H 0AD

Printed and Bound in Great Britain by
Billing & Sons Limited, Guildford and London

INTRODUCTION

These S.U. Bible Study aids take the place of the *Bible Study Notes* which have enjoyed consistent, wide circulation since they first appeared in 1947. They are therefore being published at regular intervals so that they can be used for personal daily Bible study by those who formerly took the *Notes*.

Each volume is divided into the right number of sections to make daily use possible, though dates are not attached to the sections because the books will have a continuing use as a simple Bible commentary.

With this in mind, the books of the Bible have been so divided up that, when the series is complete, the subscriber will have a complete Bible Commentary, with the books of the Bible in Biblical order.

Normally each volume will provide material for one quarter's use, with between 92 and 96 sections (the authors have been commissioned to divide the material according to the best exegetical pattern for this purpose). Where it is suggested that two sections should be read together in order to fit the three-month period, they are marked with an asterisk.

Because of the special problem created by the book of Psalms, which obviously ought to be in one volume, and the Gospel of Mark, which is so much shorter than the other Gospels, the pattern of volumes in the second year is different from the rest. The Psalms are dealt with in a four-month unit, and Mark in a two-month unit. Similarly, the books immediately preceding Psalms in the Bible are a two-month unit, and 1 and 2 Corinthians with Galatians a four-month unit. Otherwise, all the volumes are designed to give one quarter's readings.

The scheme as a whole will be completed in five years, and overleaf is a chart showing how it is planned.

In this series, it is assumed that the reader will be using one of the standard editions of the RSV (or one of the 'Study Bibles' based on it), and will therefore have the marginal references and footnotes of that Bible available; many of these references will not be repeated in these books, and users are therefore recommended to look up the RSV references as a regular part of their daily study. If the RSV is not available, then the use of the Revised Version, American Standard Version, or a good marginal reference Authorized (King James') Version is recommended.

	1967	1968	1969	1970	1971
First Quarter	St. Luke	Psalms (four-month course)	St. John	1 and 2 Peter 1, 2 and 3 John Jude Revelation	St. Matthew
Second Quarter	Joshua Judges Ruth 1 & 2 Samuel	St. Mark	Proverbs Ecclesiastes Song of Solomon Isaiah 1–39	Lamentations Ezekiel Daniel	Genesis Exodus
Third Quarter	Acts	1 and 2 Corinthians Galatians (four-month course)	Ephesians Philippians Colossians 1 and 2 Thessalonians	1 and 2 Timothy and Titus Philemon Hebrews James	Romans
Fourth Quarter	1 and 2 Kings 1 and 2 Chronicles	Ezra Nehemiah Esther Job	Isaiah 40–66 Jeremiah	Hosea Joel Amos Obadiah Jonah Micah Nahum Habakkuk Zephaniah Haggai Zechariah Malachi	Leviticus Numbers Deuteronomy

1 Timothy, 2 Timothy, Titus

INTRODUCTION

These three writings are known in modern times by the collective title the 'Pastoral Epistles'. They contain material of use to pastors, and are concerned with the immediate practical problems confronting the Christian in a pastoral situation. As they stand they give guidance to Timothy and Titus, two of Paul's assistants, as to how they should handle the problems involved in their oversight of churches. These men were, of course, not pastors of individual groups of Christians, but rather superintendents of pastors whose sphere was much wider.

Nowhere in antiquity is there any indication that the general character of these letters was doubted. It was accepted that they were genuine letters of Paul and that they were written to the two recipients mentioned. But in modern times both conclusions are often doubted. It is held that the letters were written, probably early in the second century, by some orthodox believer, anxious to perpetuate Paul's teaching as he understood it, and only conventionally addressed to Timothy and Titus. The principal reasons for holding such views are first, linguistic (the language of these three letters is held to be so different from that of the ten 'genuine' Pauline letters that they must come from a different author) and secondly, doctrinal (the Pastorals are said to be concerned with doctrines which were of no concern to Paul while, conversely, characteristic Pauline doctrines are passed over).

It may be significant that few critics care to commit themselves to the view that there is nothing Pauline about our three letters. They usually hold that there are some genuine Pauline fragments which a later writer has taken and written up. It may be accepted that there is something Pauline about them. And a number of competent critics are convinced that the objections to Pauline authorship of the whole will not stand up to critical examination. For the view that the letters are late and non-Pauline see the Introductions to the commentaries by C. K. Barrett and A. T. Hanson, and for the Pauline view those by J. N. D. Kelly and D. Guthrie.

In these studies we will treat the letters as genuine Pauline products, written with a desire to convey to Paul's younger assistants guidance for the oversight of the churches.

As to their date, the biographical details which emerge incidentally make it impossible in the judgement of most scholars to fit them into the period covered by *Acts*. It seems that Paul was released from the imprisonment mentioned at the end of that book and engaged in further missionary activity. The Pastorals belong to this late period.

1 Timothy 1.1-11 — The Lawful Use of the Law

A first-century letter usually began with the name of the writer, a short description of him, the name of the recipient(s) with a similar brief description, and a little prayer. Paul breathes life into this conventional framework by making it the means of bringing out important Christian teaching. Here we see something of the nature of apostleship (a man does not say, 'I think I'll be an apostle'; he must first be commanded by God and Christ), the close relationship between God and Christ (none else could be joined together as they are), the tender relationship between Paul and his convert Timothy, and the primacy of qualities like grace, mercy, and peace. Paul usually has grace and peace in his greetings, but in his two letters to Timothy 'mercy' is included as well.

In the letter proper, the first thing emphasized is the importance of sound doctrine issuing in upright living. 'The law is good,' Paul says, 'if any one uses it lawfully' (8). It is for the restraint of wickedness of all kinds (9 f.). This might be put in another way, as when Paul speaks of the aim of his charge to Timothy as love (5). The use of both ideas shows that he is not arguing for the kind of 'situational ethics' dear to some modern thinkers. He agrees that love is the important attitude for a Christian, and that it proceeds 'from a pure heart and a good conscience and sincere faith' (5). But this does not mean that the law can be disregarded. Elsewhere Paul tells us that 'love is the fulfilling of the law' (Rom. 13.10) and this is much the thought here. This is not in contradiction of the gospel, but in accordance with it (11). And it is something given, something entrusted, to Paul (11) and indeed to all Christians.

But it is always easier to get into an argument than to live the Christian life. It is human nature to prefer vigorous discussion to sacrificial living. 'Certain persons' (3) whom Timothy confronted were using the law the wrong way. Evidently they were using some form of allegorical interpretation which made the Bible yield 'myths and endless genealogies' (4); they had 'wandered away into vain discussion' (6). It is still quite possible to use the Bible not as the source of 'the divine training that is in faith' (4), but as the starting point for the exposition of our own pet theories. Calling these 'Christian' or 'orthodox' or 'sound doctrine' does not make them so. For that there must be a real subjection to what God has revealed.

4

Wonder at the miracle of grace which changed Saul the persecutor of the Church into Paul the apostle of Jesus Christ never left this transformed sinner. The mention of the gospel with which he has been entrusted (11) immediately recalls to his mind what that gospel meant in his own experience. He had 'blasphemed and persecuted and insulted' Christ. His conversion did not represent a minor change in a man who was fairly well disposed to things Christian. It represented God's miracle in the heart of a deeply guilty man. Both the guilt and the miracle were real. There is always a tendency for Christ's followers to limit the power of God. Without ever putting it into words we frequently act as though we expect conversions only among those who have the right background and upbringing. While we should never undervalue the importance of good early training nor the way God so often uses this to bring about spiritual depth, we should not regard it as the indispensable preliminary to a real conversion. The miracle of Paul has been repeated many times in the history of the Church, not least in our own day.

Out of this two important lessons emerge. The first is that the salvation of sinners was the purpose of the coming of Jesus into the world (15). 'He did not only come to seek; it was to save He came.' The second is that God uses whatever experiences a man has before his conversion as well as those afterwards. Paul received mercy 'for this reason', that Christ's work in him might be an example. Every converted sinner has that in his background which now redounds to the glory of God no matter how little credit it was to the sinner when he did it.

Notes: V. 13: 'blasphemed and persecuted and insulted' translates three nouns, 'blasphemer and persecutor and insolent man'. That he acted 'ignorantly in unbelief' is not the reason for Paul's being saved, but it is a mitigating circumstance. He had even then acted 'with a clear conscience' (2 Tim. 1.3). Notice that he does not exaggerate his sinfulness. V. 14: 'overflowed' translates a strong term giving the thought of lavish and abundant supply. V. 15: 'The saying is sure and worthy' renders a Greek expression (*pistos ho logos*) found only in the Pastorals (1 Tim. 3.1; 4.9; 2 Tim. 2.11; Tit. 3.8). It marks the saying as both important and reliable. Paul's humility comes out at the end of the verse. V. 17: typically Paul's gratitude finds expression in a little outburst of praise. 'The King of the ages' (RV margin) is found only here in the N.T. (unless it be read in Rev. 15.3). It is a strong affirmation of God's eternity.

Paul's testimony to God's grace at work in him is not an idle tale. He means Timothy to be inspired by what God has done in him, so that he too may go on to fulfil all God's purpose in his own life. God has important work for Timothy to do and it is important that he should not fail to accomplish it. There is dispute about the meaning of 'the prophetic utterances which pointed to you' (18), and some see a reference to Timothy's ordination, calling attention to 4.14. But perhaps more relevant is Acts 13.1–3, which speaks of the work of the Holy Spirit in initiating the travels of Barnabas and Paul which were to lead the apostles to Timothy. Cf. NEB, 'that prophetic utterance which first pointed you out to me.' Either way Paul is stressing the divine initiative in calling men to any work of ministry. Timothy should obey the charge not because on the purely human level he has started a work and ought to finish it (true though that might be), but because God has designated him for a piece of service which he dare not fail to accomplish. Paul is able to point to a certain Hymenaeus and Alexander who have rejected the leading of their conscience and who accordingly have 'made shipwreck of their faith' (19).

After this build-up it is perhaps surprising that the very first duty Paul lays upon Timothy is that of prayer, particularly prayer for rulers and all in positions of authority. But prayer is not the tepid, insipid thing that modern Christians have so often made it. It is an adventure with God. It is a powerful weapon for the waging of our warfare in the world. It is the believer's one effectual means of bringing about mighty results. And this is not to be confined to what we would call 'spiritual' things. The issues of community life concern the Christian as much as they concern any member of the community. But whereas his unbelieving brother usually does no more than complain about those set over him, the Christian can, and must, pray for them. In his prayers he is a partner with them and sets forward right purposes.

Notes: V. 20: The meaning of 'delivered to Satan' (cf. 1 Cor. 5.5) is not clear, but it involves disciplinary action and probably supernatural punishment. 2.4: God's will is for salvation, not that men be lost. V. 6: 'ransom' (*antilutron*) points to the substitutionary nature of Christ's offering of Himself.

Meditation: Three key doctrines of the Christian faith are found in vs. 5,6—the unity of the Godhead, the mediatorship of Christ, the atoning sacrifice of the cross.

1 Timothy 2.8-15 Woman's Place

The respective places of the sexes have been a problem from the very beginning. It is clear that in the early Church there were some women who felt that the fact that 'there is neither male nor female; for you are all one in Christ Jesus' (Gal. 3.28) abolished all distinctions between the sexes. They were emancipated, and could do anything at all that men could do. Paul deals with the topic more than once. He maintains that before God there is no room for a superior sex. All are equal in His sight. But that does not mean that the functions to be discharged by the two are identical. The sexes are cast for different roles, and, while full allowance should be made for exceptional cases, neither should try to usurp the functions of the other.

On this occasion his subject is public worship. Men should pray everywhere, he says. 'Lifting holy hands' reminds us that posture for prayer is not without significance. The Bible does not prescribe any one posture, but as we pray we should be aware that our attitude of body is not without influence on our attitude of mind. 'Without anger or quarrelling' spells out the importance of right inward attitudes. We cannot pray effectively when filled with concern for our own petty vindication. It is likely that we should take the sense of v. 9 from the previous verse, 'that women likewise should pray, dressed in seemly apparel'. Paul's first point is that women should set more store by their manner of life than their manner of dress (9 f.; this does not mean that they should not dress attractively, it is an insistence that the priorities be right). His second is that a woman should not take a place of superiority over her husband (12; 'men' [RSV] is singular, and it is the usual word for 'husband', though it can on occasion mean 'man'). He drives this home by an appeal to the case of Adam who was 'not deceived' by Satan in the way Eve was. He simply followed her, but her fall came about through assuming an unwarranted place of leadership. V. 15 might mean that women will be 'brought safely through childbirth' (NEB margin), or 'saved' in the sense of finding fulfilment and a proper place in life through bearing children. The man who has just written vs. 5 f. cannot be held to mean that eternal salvation is won by childbirth.

Thought: The conditions of effectual praying are purity (selfward), peace (manward), faith (Godward). (A. M. Stibbs on v. 8.)

7

1 Timothy 3.1-7

Paul's second 'sure saying' (cf. **1**.15) emphasizes the nobility of Christian service. He is speaking specifically about the 'bishop', who, most competent scholars agree, is to be equated with 'presbyter' (cf. Tit. **1**.5–9). 'Bishop' stresses the thought of oversight, as 'presbyter' that of seniority. These officials exercised leadership in the early Church, and from their functions there emerged in due course the offices of presbyter and bishop as we know them in the later Church (I have discussed this more fully in *Ministers of God*, ch. V). At this early stage in the Church's history, Paul's prime concern is that those who so exercise leadership should be men whose lives agree with their teaching. Notice the importance attached to home life (2,4 f.). It is an interesting provision that the bishop must not be a recent convert (6): maturity in faith is important for all who exercise any function of leadership. Paul also attaches importance to the way the Church's leadership is seen from outside (7). If the bishop does not have a good reputation there is danger. The devil will catch him and that will be greatly to the disadvantage of all that he stands for. He himself will be harmed and so will the Church.

Study: In view of conditions created by contemporary society, list in order of immediate importance the bishop's qualifications and duties found in these verses. To what extent are these demands met in your local church? Should church officers be appointed if no one fulfils these high standards exactly?

1 Timothy 3.8-13

It appears that in the early Church the staple of the local ministry was bishops and deacons (apostles, prophets, and others exercised wider ministries and cannot be thought part of the local organization). So after speaking of the bishop Paul turns his attention to the deacons. Between two sets of instructions specifically addressed to deacons (8–10, 12 f.) there is another for 'the women' (11). Some hold this to refer to the wives of the deacons, others to deaconesses. The principal point in favour of the former is that there is little clear evidence in the N.T. of a specific order of deaconess, or for that matter in the early Church. In favour of the latter is the difficulty of seeing why Paul should take two bites at the deacon's duties interspersed with an instruction that does not concern a church official. On the whole it seems more likely that he does refer to deaconesses. As in the case of bishops, deacons must be people of good character. They must have a sense of serious purpose, be careful of their speech and indulge themselves neither in wine nor in gain. A firm hold on the faith is important (9) and it is important that they be tested before being admitted to office. Unfortunately Paul does not tell us in what the test consisted, nor for that matter in what the office consisted. We are left to guess at both. We do not know what deacons did in those early days. There is a reference to the deacon's home life (12) and to the result of serving well (13).

Notes: V. 8: Deacons are to be 'serious' (*semnos*) as are the women (11); and for that matter the bishops, (4); the same root is there rendered 'respectful'. The term denotes a sense of high and serious purpose, the opposite of frivolity. V. 9: 'mystery' means something that men cannot possibly work out for themselves (not simply that which is difficult to work out), and usually, as here, there is the added thought that it has now been revealed. Men would never have guessed that the way of salvation has nothing to do with their good living, prayers, offerings, etc., but that it depended on God's sending His Son to die for us. That had to be revealed. V. 11: 'slanderers' is literally 'devils'. Let us not take slanderous gossip lightly as though it were a normal part of human life. It is not. It is devilish.

1 Timothy 3.14—4.5   The Faith—and its Perversion

At the end of ch. 3 we have a poetic expression which may well have formed part of a Christian hymn. The arrangement in the RSV brings out the rhythmical structure, though it is not certain that this precise form should be followed (it could be three couplets or simply six lines). 'He' (16) at the beginning is properly 'who' or 'He who' (see margin; some manuscripts read 'God' but 'He who' seems correct). This is not explained but there is no doubt but that Jesus Christ is meant. The hymn then refers to His incarnation, then apparently to His resurrection. It was this that the Spirit used to bring about His vindication (cf. Rom. 1.4). 'Seen by angels' may refer to the same thing, for angels saw Him at the resurrection. But it may well be the ascension that is primarily in mind at this point. There is uncertainty about the last line. This may be another reference to the ascension, but it makes good sense to see it as used prophetically of the final triumph. Then the six lines of the hymn would represent six stages arranged chronologically. This is a magnificent statement of the sweep of Christ's saving work.

But some are not content with it, and Paul moves immediately to those who 'will depart from the faith' (4.1). That the Spirit 'expressly says' this indicates that what is to take place is not beyond God's control. He is supreme despite the ragings of men and their preference for 'deceitful spirits and doctrines of demons' (4.1). The heretics in mind are wrong in three ways: (i) Their doctrine is astray as we have seen. (ii) Their conscience is also astray (2). (iii) Their attitude to the things God has created is astray (3). In the ancient world as in the modern men sometimes advocated celibacy for religious reasons. Some also drew up curious food laws. Paul insists that both are completely wrong, for there is nothing God has created which is to be rejected if it is received in the proper way (4.4 f.).

Notes: V. 15: Note the dignity of the Church and its place in God's scheme of things. V. 16: 'mystery' again, the essence of 'our religion' is not of human origin but has been revealed by God. 4.4 f.: control of diet for proper reasons is not in question. Paul is opposing the erection of food laws for religious reasons. The Christian knows no such taboos. V. 3: Paul is not saying that none is called to serve God in the unmarried state (cf. 1 Cor. 7.7), but that celibacy is not in principle to be exalted above marriage.

Questions for further study and discussion on 1 Timothy 1.1—4.5

1. What is the place of the O.T. in the life of the Christian?
2. Bearing in mind 1.12–16 and 4.1–5 discuss the relationship between a right faith and right conduct.
3. What place should the believer be taking in the life of his community?
4. How can Paul's teaching on women be applied to the modern situation, especially in situations like the mission field?
5. How do Paul's criteria for bishops and deacons apply to the ministry of the modern church and to the service of lay people?

1 Timothy 4.6-11   Training in Godliness

That we simply grow in the Christian faith by doing nothing about it is a crazy notion. Paul has already pointed out that the devil is active and eager to trip up even Christian leaders (3.7). Now he develops the theme that it is important for the servants of God to train themselves in godliness (7). There is always the temptation to erect any rules that may be devised by Christians into a system which must at any cost be complied with. It is even easy to slip into the error of thinking that our systems enable us to acquire merit before God. When such attitudes occur our systems are a snare. But that does not mean that we should go to the opposite extreme and simply drift through life. We must be nourished (6). We must be trained (7). We must toil and strive (10). It is very helpful for the believer to work out a rule of life whereby he engages in the kind of reading, prayer, worship, and the like, which will build him up in the faith. There is no one way of doing this. To lay down rules binding on all Christians would be a calamitous error. But, human nature being what it is, for the average Christian settled habits, especially of prayer and Bible study, are tremendously important.

The Christian is nourished on 'the words of the faith' and of 'good doctrine' (6). This means that study of the Bible and of Christian doctrine are a necessity. The fact that we do this will in itself put us off 'godless and silly myths' (7). Perversions of the faith abound. But the Christian who is nourished in the Word of God and in sound doctrine will not readily fall a prey to them. We are familiar with the value of physical exercise for the development of physical fitness. Paul brings out the point that there is a spiritual analogy (8). He goes further, for he points out that training in godliness is of value not only in the here and now, but also 'for the life to come'. What folly accordingly to neglect it! He solemnly assures Timothy of the importance of this (9) and rounds off the section with the reminder that all this is worth doing because our hope is set on God. When Paul speaks of God as 'the Saviour of all men, especially of those who believe' he is not saying that all men will be saved ultimately and that believers will be specially saved. He is saying that God watches over all men, delivering them from evils and showering His blessings on them. He makes His sun shine on all and sends rain on just and unjust alike (Matt. 5.45). But 'Saviour' has a fuller, richer, and deeper meaning for men who believe. They are saved in a way other men are not.

1 Timothy 4.12-16   An Example to Follow

Student unrest, protests, and even riots, in many lands mean that modern youth is in no danger of over-submissiveness. 'Let no one despise your youth' (12) is scarcely a necessary injunction for our generation, no matter how much Timothy needed it. Young people as a whole are very confident, at least in their criticism of the 'establishment'.

But even modern youth may well ask itself 'Exactly what am I trying to do? What kind of life am I seeking to establish?' Paul reminds Timothy that men do not live unto themselves. Inevitably their lives form some sort of example. What sort is the important thing. Both 'speech and conduct' are important, and Paul looks for a lead 'in love, in faith, in purity'. All three are important in a

11

world like ours and doubly so among rebellious youth. Timothy was a public figure in the Church and Paul goes on to consider how he should discharge his responsibilities. It is interesting that in the conduct of worship he singles out public reading of Scripture, preaching, and teaching (13). It is still the case that these are the significant elements in worship. Christian worship must centre on the reading of Scripture, for it is rooted in what God has revealed in Christ. And the preaching which sets forth the teachings of Scripture is a necessary consequence. 'Teaching' is not so very different from preaching, but it puts some emphasis on instruction in sound doctrine. It is not a matter of indifference what is taught in the name of Christ. A little later Paul stresses this again: 'Take heed to yourself and to your teaching' (16). In a day when many conflicting views are put forward as authentic Christianity it is well to give attention once more to the content of teaching. Scripture affords our standard, and that which does not agree with the revelation is not accepted.

Paul further exhorts his young friend, 'Do not neglect the gift you have' (14). It is easy to sigh for gifts we do not possess and in the process neglect the one God has given us. In Timothy's case Paul is apparently referring to ordination, for that is the natural interpretation of the laying on of the hands of the elders. Fulfilment of any ministry is not automatic, but requires diligent effort.

Notes: V. 16: 'save' is used in a wide sense of realizing to the full what is implicit in the Christian salvation.

1 Timothy 5.1-8   Honour where Honour is Due

Paul turns to classes of people in the church and instructs Timothy in the proper attitudes to be taken up towards them. He begins with the 'older man' or perhaps the 'elder' (it is not always certain whether the term is being used of age or of official position; but the official appears in v. 17, so that here we probably have senior citizens). It is not proper for a youth to rebuke his elders. Timothy should therefore treat older men as he would his father. This gives the clue to the way the Christian should interpret all his relationships within the community of believers. He should treat fellow Christians as brothers, mothers or sisters (1 f.).

It seems clear that in the early Church there was a sustained attempt to relieve the needs of widows (cf. Acts 6.1 for the early origin of the practice). Due to the social customs of the day they were in a particularly vulnerable position and the church saw their care as something important. But the financial resources of the church were very limited, and it was important that they be used wisely. This appears to be behind vs. 3 ff., with the distinction between 'real widows' and others. Paul enjoins family piety. People should make provision for their own where they can (4; cf. v. 16). It seems not unlikely that when the church began to help the needy widows some who were far from worthy tried to get on the list. So Paul speaks of the kind of life that a 'real widow' will live. He contrasts her dependence on God and her constant prayers with the self-indulgence of one who 'is dead even while she lives' (5 f.). And Paul can use very strong language when he comes to the importance of making proper provision for one's own immediate family (8). This is not the kind of thing to be left to the collective efforts of the church where one can well do it oneself. Even unbelievers will often perform this duty and in so doing show up the professing Christian who does not. 'He has disowned the faith' is a strong statement and should provoke serious reflection.

1 Timothy 5.9-16 Young Widows

Paul continues with the problem of widows. First he speaks of enrolling mature widows whose lives commend the faith. Presumably this means putting them on an official list of people who would be given financial or other assistance, and who apparently would be expected to do something to forward the work of the church. The widow who qualifies is over sixty years of age, has been 'faithful in marriage to one man' (9, NEB; this cannot mean 'having been the wife of one husband' [RSV], for Paul goes on to commend second marriage, v. 14), and has lived an exemplary life.

Younger widows are a different proposition. From v. 12 it seems that being 'enrolled' meant pledging oneself to some form of service which involved continuance in the unmarried state. Young widows naturally looked forward to remarriage in due course, and this made it difficult for them to fulfil their pledge. While they were doing service it would be with a divided mind, for some of their attention would be concentrated on their own future marriage. And if they did marry, the pledge to continue in that service would be broken. Paul is not blaming them for a desire for remarriage. On the contrary, he expressly encourages it (14). But he is realistic enough to see the effect of their natural desires on their performance of the duties expected of those on the roll. Moreover, lack of maturity may lead them to indulge in gossip when they think they are engaged in visiting (13). Paul was a very practical person! On all counts it was better that they be not enrolled.

13

Over against this Paul sets the desirable procedure. These young widows should by all means remarry (14). This would give each a proper place in a household and an important task to perform. Instead of being the targets for legitimate criticism they would then give no occasion for 'the enemy' to gain an entrance. Paul makes it clear that he is speaking out of experience. Some had already made the most grievous error by straying after Satan (15). The reference in the concluding verse to 'any believing woman' is somewhat puzzling as one would have thought the duty of providing for one's own family rested on male Christians as well as on women. Probably Paul means that if there are widows in a household they will come under the immediate care of the housewife. Thus she should 'assist them'. The church can then concentrate its aid on those who are really destitute.

Thought: V. 14: 'The greatest gift of Christianity to the social fabric is the development of the idea of home' (G. Matheson).

1 Timothy 5.17-25   The Ministry of Elders

The exact functions of the elders are not set out in the N.T. But we may assume that they were not dissimilar to those exercised by the synagogue elders, in which case the elders were the responsible local officials. Here we learn that they (or at least some of them) 'ruled' and that some laboured 'in preaching and teaching'. The implication from the latter statement is that some did not preach or teach. They were to be remunerated for their work (18), and esteemed as reverend personages, not lightly to be accused (19). But this does not mean that they were not to be accused under any circumstances. They might on occasion do wrong, and the persistent sinner must be rebuked publicly (20). Precisely because they were leaders and very much in the public eye, wrongdoing on their part must not be condoned. So Timothy is warned against respect of persons (21).

In its context the reference to 'the laying on of hands' (22) must refer to ordination (cf. 4.14). This is a very important act, and must be exercised with due care. To ordain a man who is not worthy is to be responsible for the harm that will follow; it means participating in the sins of another. At the end of our passage another aspect of sin is emphasized, namely, that in the end sin will out. Sometimes sin appears hidden, sometimes obvious. But nothing can prevent final disclosure. It is comforting to reflect that the same is true of goodness (25).

There is a little health note (23). The ancients did not know that germs in the water supply could cause disease, and they were ignorant of the fact that the alcohol in wine killed them. But they normally drank nothing but water or wine, and they observed that people who drank water only, sometimes got diseases that those who used wine did not. It is this which is behind Paul's injunction. In our day, when there is a multiplicity of beverages and when the causes of sickness are better known, it is possible to get the required result without resorting to the use of wine.

Notes: V. 17: 'honour' is usually taken to mean or at least include the thought of remuneration ('stipend', NEB). V. 18: Note the linking as 'Scripture' of verses from Deut. 25.4 and Matt. 10.10 (or Luke 10.7).

Thought: The ministry especially worthy of 'double honour' (17) is that of preaching and teaching. Consider the implications of this fact.

1 Timothy 6.1-2   Slaves

Slaves presented a problem to the early Church. On the one hand slavery was an institution accepted throughout the world, and probably no one envisaged a society in which there could be no slaves at all. But on the other, there was that in Christianity which was incompatible with slavery and which meant that in time those who took their faith seriously must do away with this monstrous system. Believing slaves were regarded by Christians from the very first as brothers in Christ. They were men for whom Christ died, and they were redeemed just as truly as any free man. So Paul can understand the unity of believers in Christ to mean among other things that 'there is neither slave nor free' (Gal. 3.28). He can speak of a slave as 'a beloved brother' of his owner (Philem. 16).

Now to some slaves this must have been heady teaching. Accustomed all their lives to being treated as no better than cattle, to being bought and sold in the market place, to being chattels for their masters' use, it was an intoxicating thought that they were their masters' equals in God's sight. It was only to be expected that some in this new-found faith were inclined to presume on their new relationship. Especially when their masters were Christians they found it difficult to retain their ordinary station. And this in turn must have been something of a hindrance to the gospel. If becoming a Christian meant putting up with disrespect from slaves and finding them less ready to work than where the owners were heathen, some-slave owners would not even consider the claims of the gospel.

15

Thus in the N.T. from time to time there are warnings to slaves not to presume on their new relationship to their masters. In our present passage Paul is pointing out that slaves should give their owners due respect. Indeed they should serve all the more willingly in that those who receive the benefit of their labours are themselves believers.

1 Timothy 6.3-10 Misinterpreting the Faith

Paul comes back to the thought of false teaching which he has already opposed (4.1 ff.). It is important that we take Christianity for what it is and not impose our own pattern on it, making it what we wish it to be. That is the way of pride (4), the way which in effect means (whatever its exponents may say) that those who put it forth know better than Christ and His apostles. A concern for orthodox teaching does not come simply from an innate conservatism. It comes from a firm conviction that there is a finality about God's sending of His Son. Men cannot improve on the teaching of the Son of God or on that which He committed to His apostles. The apostles bore the definitive witness to Jesus and to reject this is to walk the way of pride and self-sufficiency. The false teachers Paul has in mind also had a love for controversy. Discussion of issues can be a useful way of clearing up the points involved. But it can degenerate into 'disputes about words' and result in angry wrangling (4 f.).

Mixed in with the heretical teaching was a concern for material profit. Regrettably throughout the centuries there have been those who have used religion as a means of personal profit, and the sorry story is not yet over. Paul points out that to imagine that 'godliness is a means of gain' is to be 'depraved in mind and bereft of the truth' (5). But this enables him to make the point that godliness does indeed bring gain, though of a very different sort than money. The end of our passage is a discussion of the way in which the love of money can harm spiritual life. This should be closely studied in an age as materialistic as our own. It is the case that men will often retain their faith in the face of difficulties and even persecutions, but surrender it in the piping days of peace and prosperity. The love of money and all it brings is an insidious thing. It can and does corrupt the most unlikely people, and bring in its train all kinds of evils (10).

Notes: V. 9: 'desire to be rich' means 'set their will on being rich'. V. 10: 'all evils' means 'every kind of evil' not 'all the evil there is'.

For self-examination: 'Content' (8). Does this describe my inner feelings today in regard to what I possess, what I have achieved, and what I want? How far should it?

1 Timothy 6.11-21   The Good Fight of Faith

Paul concludes his letter with a renewed call to Timothy to engage in strenuous Christian service, and with special warnings for the rich and the knowledgeable. It is never easy to be a Christian, and believers must always be alert against temptation to think that they will grow in spiritual maturity and judgement by the simple device of sitting still. There are some things that can be learned only in quietness and waiting on the Lord. There is 'a time to keep silence' as well as 'a time to speak' (Eccl. 3.7). But it is also the case that God has called His servants to work for Him in a busy world, a world where evil abounds and where it is easy to find excuses for avoiding difficult courses of action. So Paul can exhort Timothy, 'Fight the good fight of the faith' (12). The devil is often likened to an enemy, one who takes hostile action against the people of God. It is important to be clear that our battle is a real one and that it calls for our best endeavour in the strength of Christ. Paul appeals to Timothy's call and to 'the good confession' he made before many (12). Some understood this to refer to his baptism, but it seems more likely to refer to ordination. Paul reminds Timothy that his solemn confession had been made before God and Christ (who Himself made 'the good confession'), so it is not to be regarded lightly.

The apostle has some words for the rich (17–19). They are tempted above most men to rely on what is at best temporary and uncertain, and need help in getting their priorities right. They still need help, as do those who put their confidence in 'what is falsely called knowledge' (20). Undue preoccupation with what appears to be knowledge can be damaging to faith.

Question: What are the marks of a 'man of God' indicated in vs. 11,12?

Questions for further study and discussion on 1 Timothy 4.6—6.21
1. How can Paul's injunction to Timothy to set an example (4.12) be applied to your own situation?
2. What relevance has Paul's teaching on widows to the modern church?
3. In the light of Paul's teaching on slavery (6.1 f.) discuss the role of the Christian in social change.

4. What does Paul teach us in these chapters about the right use of material possessions?
5. Paul says a good deal about false teaching and about knowledge (e.g. 4.6 f., 6.3 ff., 20 f.). In days when men know so much and esteem knowledge so highly, how may we apply his words?

2 Timothy 1.1-5   Thanksgiving

As with *1 Timothy*, Paul opens this letter in the conventional way, but he adapts the conventional framework in order to bring out Christian teaching. He speaks of his apostolate as 'by the will of God' and also as 'according to the promise of the life which is in Christ Jesus' (1). God does not send His apostles aimlessly. He has a definite plan, and they move according to that plan, a plan which concerns the bringing of life to sinful man. The word 'promise' is a reminder that life comes as God's gift. It is not earned by human merit. Paul strikes a note of tenderness when he refers to Timothy as 'my beloved child' (2). Clearly Timothy was very dear to him.

As we turn to Paul's opening thanksgiving we may profitably reflect that this is a necessary part of the Christian life. The ungrateful Christian is a contradiction in terms. All that is necessary in order to come up with matter for thanksgiving is a good memory. So Paul now remembers that his ancestors had served God 'with a clear conscience' (3) and he is following in their steps. The Christian faith he professed was not a recent invention but the fulfilment of all that was involved in the religion of his forefathers. He worshipped the same God as they, and did it with complete sincerity. Paul is able to recall also that Timothy had cause for similar thanksgiving, for his mother and his grandmother had been women of faith, that faith which Timothy himself now possessed (5). While we cannot trust to the merits of our predecessors in the faith, it is always good to recall them and to thank God for them.

The tears of which Paul writes (4) were evidently tears shed by Timothy when they parted. There were not the same inhibitions in those days about men weeping as in the modern western world. This is evidence not of weakness but of affection.

A point to ponder: Paul uses three different expressions for remembering in vs. 3,4,5 (and another in v. 6). Memory is important and many-sided.

2 Timothy 1.6-14   The Pattern of the Sound Words

Arising out of the goodly heritage in which Timothy stood, Paul proceeds to exhort him to faithfulness in his ministry. It is usual to take the gift given by the laying on of Paul's hands (6) as the divine enablement given at Timothy's ordination (cf. 1 Tim. 4.14), though some prefer a reference to an equivalent of confirmation. The point in either case is that God's gifts do not operate automatically and quite irrespective of men's spiritual states and inclinations. Such gifts must be 'stirred up' if they are to be effective.

Much of our passage is concerned with the necessity for boldness in Christian witness and ministry (7,8,12). In every age it has been easier to be timid than to stand up and be counted for Christ. And in every age men have needed the uncompromising message of what God has done in Christ for their salvation. It is still important that Christians be ashamed neither of the gospel by which they stand nor of their fellow Christians with whom they stand (cf. v.8). This will often involve a measure of suffering, but then that is inseparable from the life of the Christian (3.12), and especially from that of the preacher (11 f.).

The other great thought before us is that of the given nature of the Christian message. Notice the way the thought of what God has given runs through our passage (6,7,9,12,14). God gave the gift of salvation, in all its many sidedness. But He has entrusted the proclamation of that full and rich salvation to men. They are not to try to improve on it. They are to proclaim it.

Notes: V. 7: notice the importance of self-control and the company it keeps. V. 12: 'my deposit' might be 'that which I have committed unto Him,' but the RSV is probably correct. The same word 'deposit' is found in v. 14.

Meditation: Trace in vs. 9–11 our past salvation, our future hope, our present duty.

2 Timothy 1.15—2.13   Endurance for Christ

The theme running through this passage is the importance of being single-minded in our service of Christ. It is not easy to be a Christian and never has been. So active is the opposition that it comes naturally to a man like Paul to use military terms for Christian service. Thus here he speaks of being 'a good soldier of Christ Jesus' (2.3). The metaphor has point.

Paul first brings this out by drawing attention to a couple of citizens who fell short (1.15) and to one who did not (1.16 ff.). The time of testing sifts men. It is not to be taken for granted that a man who starts out hopefully on the path of service will continue. These two did not. From this Paul turns to direct exhortation to Timothy to 'be strong in the grace that is in Christ Jesus' (2.1).

Then he borrows illustrations from three different spheres of human endeavour to drive home his point that endurance to the end is a necessity. The soldier does not entangle himself in civilian affairs. The athlete must strive lawfully (which involves strict training). The farmer must work hard before partaking of the fruits of his labour.

Paul is qualified to exhort his young friend, for he is practising what he preaches. He is no arm-chair strategist, giving good advice in the knowledge that he himself will not be hurt. He writes from prison (2.9) and speaks from a wealth of experience, much of it painful, which gave him full and accurate knowledge of what being a good soldier of Christ means.

It is generally held that 2.11–13 is part of an early Christian hymn, and that the words 'The saying is sure' refer to the following, not the preceding. The point of the hymn in this context is that it forms an encouragement to troubled Christians. It speaks of the certainty of ultimate vindication for those who serve Christ faithfully (11,12a). It reminds us of the grim certainty that will follow a denial of Christ (cf. Matt. 10.33). But the hymn ends on a note of assurance. God is faithful, and His faithfulness will persist. This is not a charter for laxity of service, but an encouragement to troubled souls, despairing of their ability to do what they should. Their security rests not on their abilities but on God's faithfulness.

Meditation: The believer's strength is unmerited, since it is 'in . . . grace'; but it is also unlimited, since it is 'in Christ Jesus'.

2 Timothy 2.14-19   God's Workman

Paul is fond of contrasting mere words with real power (e.g. 1 Cor. 2.4; 4.19 f.; 1 Thess. 1.5). When a man becomes a Christian this means more than mere outward profession. It is true that what the Christian says is important. He is to bear his witness to Jesus. But it is even more important that he should have a witness to bear, that he should be manifesting in his life the power of the Spirit of God. It is in this spirit that Paul urges Timothy to do his best to be 'a workman who has no need to be ashamed' (15). There is nothing high-faluting about 'workman'. It is a down-to-earth word (used often of agricultural labourers), and points to the fact that honest toil is a prime requisite for Christian service. It does not matter if we have no mystic visions. It does matter if we do not produce hard work in the service of our Lord. So Paul warns Timothy once more against 'disputing about words' (14), and 'godless chatter' (16). The false teachers with whom Timothy was confronted were evidently long on talk but short on performance. It is a temptation in the way of every Christian.

Paul singles out one specific error, namely, that of holding 'that the resurrection is past already' (18). This could doubtless be made to look superficially attractive, for there is a sense in which it is true (Col. 2.12; 3.1). But clearly these teachers were affirming it in a different sense. They were interpreting it in a 'spiritual' sense which precluded any future resurrection of the body. This is the kind of error which Paul combats so magnificently in 1 Cor. 15. It must always be opposed because 'Christianity without a resurrection ceases to be a living faith' (Guthrie). The consequence of such teaching was that some were unsettled. But Paul is not dismayed. He knows that 'God's firm foundation stands' (19), and he sees this in two O.T. passages, Num. 16.5,26. His confidence is in God.

Notes: V. 14: For 'disputing about words' cf. 1 Tim. 1.4,7; 6.4,20; 2 Tim. 2.16; 3.7 f.; 4.4, Tit. 1.10; 3.9. V.1 5: 'rightly handling' (*orthotomounta*) means literally 'cutting straight' but whether the imagery is from cutting a road (Prov. 3.6, 11.5), or cutting stones, or cutting a furrow (so NEB), is not clear. In any case the stress is on 'straight' rather than 'cutting'. V. 17: Hymenaeus is probably the one mentioned in 1 Tim. 1.20.

2 Timothy 2.20-26   Vessels for Noble Use

Upright living and the proper exercise of godly discipline in the church are the topics before us. The general bearing of the illustration from the vessels in a house is clear, but the detailed application is not. In a great house vessels of wood and earthenware have their uses, and Paul would certainly not have held that the humble and ill-equipped have no place in God's scheme of things. The thought is not so much the native qualities of believers as what they do about themselves. It is as though the vessels were able to determine for themselves something of their quality. Paul is saying something rather like the metaphor of costly or shoddy materials in building, which he uses in 1 Cor. 3. So if a man 'purifies himself' he will be 'for noble use' not ignoble.

Paul develops the theme that Timothy (and others) should aim at uprightness of living and disposition (22), but this brings him to the further thought that this means refusing to associate with 'stupid, senseless controversies' (23). The proper attitude towards those in error is a matter of some difficulty. On the one hand the Lord's servant must not do or say anything to countenance the error. On the other, he is not so much concerned to win an argument

21

as to win men for Christ. He must resist the error but in such a way that he does not repel those who hold it. He must correct his opponents indeed, but 'with gentleness' (25). The aim is to deliver them from 'the snare of the devil' (26). The RSV goes on, 'after being captured by him to do his will', taking both 'him' and 'his' to refer to the devil. Both, however, might refer to God, who would then be described as He who delivers. Perhaps better is the RSV margin, which sees 'captured by him' as the devil's work, but takes 'to do his will' with 'come to know the truth', i.e. they escape the devil to do God's will.

2 Timothy 3.1-9 False Teachers Again

It is clear throughout these epistles that Paul is greatly concerned for both purity of life and purity of doctrine. He does not regard the way a Christian lives as unimportant, nor does he dismiss the opinions he holds as of no significance. It matters that he hold the true faith and that he show this by his manner of life. At this point Paul informs Timothy that 'in the last days' there will be false teaching. To the very end we must expect that there will be some who will pervert the faith. Paul is not speaking simply of men who live badly. He is talking of professing believers, men 'holding the form of religion but denying the power of it' (5). These people are characterized in the first place as 'lovers of self' (1), and much of what follows stems from that. The unhappy list in vs. 2–4 is made up of qualities which are natural enough for those dominated by selfishness.

At the beginning Paul speaks of 'the last days.' But the evils he mentions are not confined to the End, and we may suspect that he was troubled by people of this kind in his own day. Certainly this is the case in v. 6 (notice the present tense). He appears to be speaking of religious leaders, perhaps ministers, who used their influence wrongly. They captivated credulous ladies of the type who never reach a firm knowledge of the truth (6 f.). But Paul is confident that this will not get out of hand. He likens the work of the false teachers to that of Jannes and Jambres. These names do not appear in the O.T., but in a number of early writings they are the names of the Egyptian magicians who opposed Moses. It is possible that the teachers Paul opposed practised magic (someone has remarked that superstition and heresy are often connected). But his 'as (the magicians) so (the heretics)' requires no more than that they opposed the truth. Paul concludes with an assurance that 'their folly will be plain to all' (9). Their success will not last.

Notes: V. 6: 'weak women' is a contemptuous diminutive, 'little women'; 'silly' might be a better translation. 'Burdened' is 'heaped up,' a descriptive word. V. 8: 'counterfeit' = 'that has not passed the test.'

Conviction: *But this I know, all flesh shall see His glory,*
          And He shall reap the harvest He has sown,
          And some glad day His sun shall shine in splendour
          When He, the Saviour, Saviour of the world, is known.

Questions for further study and discussion on 2 Timothy 1.1—3.9

1. In the light of 1.3 ff. discuss the place of home training in the faith.
2. How far is military imagery applicable to Christian service today?
3. Discuss the relationship between the effort of man (2.1 ff.) and the faithfulness of God (2.13).
4. In what ways can we use the imagery of the ordinary to illuminate the path of Christian service (cf. 2.20 f.; 1 Cor. 1.26 ff.).
5. How far can we apply 3.1 ff. to conditions in our own day?

2 Timothy 3.10-13   Paul's Example

One of the interesting features of the Pauline correspondence is the way the apostle so confidently appeals to his own example. He can call the Thessalonians to witness 'how holy and righteous and blameless was our behaviour to you believers' (1 Thess. 2.10), and he can even say, 'you became imitators of us and of the Lord' (1 Thess. 1.6). The whole thrust of his letters is such that he cannot have meant that he was without any sin. He is too insistent on universal sinfulness for that. But he knew very well that no believer can commend the gospel he preaches unless his life agrees with his words. And Paul was wholehearted in his living out of the faith. He had given himself unreservedly to the service of Jesus Christ and he knew that he had done so. Therefore he could and did point men to his own example. In the very different circumstances under which we live we cannot use the same language about our own lives. And in any case few of us would claim that our lives meet Paul's standard. But unless we are living in such a way that if men did follow our example they would be brought closer to Christ we cannot expect to commend the gospel. The importance of upright living cannot be overestimated.

All this lies behind this section of Paul's letter. He knows that Timothy has observed his teachings and his life. He singles out his aim, his faith, patience, love and steadfastness, before coming to persecutions. It is perhaps worth pointing out that the mention of love is specially frequent in Paul's writings. We usually think of John as the apostle of love, but Paul uses the noun more than anyone else (seventy-five times out of its one hundred and sixteen N.T. occurrences). Paul is such a controversial figure that we sometimes see him as a doughty fighter, but overlook the fact that he is gripped with the importance of love.

Nor did this come from a sheltered existence, for he had to contend with tremendous difficulties. So he goes on to encourage Timothy in his troubles by pointing out that he himself had been through bitter persecutions and God had delivered him from them all (11). He goes on to make the extremely important point that this is the common lot of Christians (12). We must not expect that in an age like ours we shall escape. If our commitment to Christ is wholehearted, we must expect persecution of some kind.

Notes: V. 11: Antioch, Iconium, and Lystra were all places Paul visited early in his ministry. Was he turning Timothy's attention to what had first attracted him to Paul? V. 12: 'desire'—the word denotes an effort of will.

2 Timothy 3.14-17   The Complete Man of God

Paul goes on from his own example to what he trusts Timothy will make of it. He is very anxious to see his protégé firmly established in the faith. He draws his attention in particular to two things, his mentors in the faith and the place of holy Scripture. Paul has already alluded to the faith of Lois and Eunice (1.5), the grandmother and mother who had been Timothy's instructors in his earliest years. In view of what he has just said we cannot doubt but that he includes himself under this heading also. He had been the means of Timothy's conversion and he had started him along the Christian way. As Timothy esteemed his predecessors in the faith, so he must take with the utmost seriousness what they told him of the way.

But Paul's most important counsel concerns Scripture. From his earliest days Timothy had known the O.T., and Paul speaks of Scripture as 'able to instruct you for salvation through faith in Christ Jesus' (15). Christ is the key to all Scripture and one cannot come to salvation apart from Him. But clearly Paul regards the place of the Bible as supremely significant. He goes on to speak of it as 'inspired by God', an expression which appears to mean 'God-breathed', i.e. it is the utterance of God. Some have suggested that we should translate in some such way as 'Every inspired scripture has its use' (NEB). The objection to this is that it may be held to mean that Paul is distinguishing between inspired and non-inspired Scripture, which would be an impossible thought for him. He is saying that Scripture comes from God and that therefore it is thoroughly reliable. It is profitable in a variety of ways. In the area of doctrine it is of value positively for teaching, negatively for reproof. It is just as useful in matters of conduct, negatively for correction, and positively for training in righteousness. Thus Paul can speak of the man of God as 'complete, equipped for every good work' (17). It is still the case that no servant of God can expect to be fully equipped for the service of God unless he is well grounded in the truth of the Bible.

Question: What 'sacred writings' of the O.T. can you recall which are able to 'instruct you for salvation through faith in Christ Jesus'?

2 Timothy 4.1-5 Preach the Word

It arises out of what Paul has been saying that Timothy should be active in God's service. There is no point in having a man of God complete and equipped for every good work if he sits down and does nothing. So having pointed to that use of Scripture which will enable Timothy to become the sort of person he ought to be, Paul immediately goes on to urge him to make the utmost use of the training he has had. This is no light matter and Paul introduces it with a solemn charge before God and Christ. He characterizes Christ as Judge, which will remind Timothy that he is a responsible man. He will one day give account of himself to this Jesus before whom Paul charges him.

The content of the exhortation boils down to one pithy command: 'preach the word' (2). All else is but commentary. Today men are often filled with the importance of modern knowledge and with the necessity for Christians to be aware of the contributions of science, philosophy, and the like, to our understanding of life and of the universe in which we live. It is well in such times to remember whence the essential Christian message is derived. We must not be obscurantist, and we certainly cannot hope to preach the gospel with any prospect of success if we ignore the world in which we live or insist on using the categories of a bygone age. But it is still the case that the essence of the gospel is a given message. We are not at liberty to manipulate its terms (cf. Gal. 1.6 f.).

Paul points out that Timothy will face a time when people will prefer another message. In every age faithful preachers of the gospel have found that this is the case. There is that about the gospel which puts down men's pride, and leaves them utterly dependent on the grace of God. This does not appeal to the natural man and his ears 'itch' for someone who will flatter his ego a little more. In this frame of mind he will listen to any myth rather than the gospel. But this does not mean that the man of God is to go along with the demand. He is to be constant in following what he knows to be right. It means steadiness, and it means the enduring of suffering (cf. 3.12). But it means also that the man of God fulfils his ministry (5). And there is no greater satisfaction on earth than that.

2 Timothy 4.6-22 The Good Fight

We should not overlook the importance of the 'For' which begins this section of the letter. The reason Paul has now urged Timothy to be urgent as an evangelist and to fulfil his ministry is that he, Paul, has finished his work. He describes this first in terms of sacrifice ('already I am being poured out as a libation', i.e. a sacrificial drink offering; he uses the same metaphor in Phil. 2.17). Then he speaks of departing, after which come three further ways of looking at his life, probably all taken from the Games. The word rendered 'fight' is a technical term for competing in an event at the Games; 'the race,' of course, means a running contest (notice that Paul does not speak of having beaten others, but only of having completed the course); 'the faith' will for Paul mean the whole content of the Christian faith, but there is probably also a glance at the Games where the competing athlete must pledge himself to compete lawfully. Paul has kept the rules, so to speak, and lived out the faith for which he stood. So there awaits him 'the crown of righteousness' (8), which reminds us of the crown awarded to the successful athlete. We could understand this to mean the crown consisting in righteousness, but this is scarcely in harmony with Paul's thought that the believer is already justified or righteous in God's sight. More probably it refers to the reward to be given at the last day to the man whose righteousness has been manifested in his living, a reward which goes not to outstanding men like Paul only, but also to 'all who have loved His appearing' (8).

Notes: V. 8: 'that Day', i.e. the day of judgement; 'His appearing', probably the second advent which was longed for ('loved'), not feared. V. 10: Demas had been a trusted fellow worker (Col. 4.14; Philem. 24). V. 13: 'the books' were evidently papyri, perhaps in roll form, 'the parchments', i.e. the 'vellums', were more costly writing material. Paul does not say what was written on either, but it seems probable that Scripture was included. Some think citizenship papers or other important personal papers may also be meant. V. 16: Apparently Paul had already had a preliminary stage in his trial, but none of his friends stood by him. Despite this the Lord delivered him at that stage (v. 17), which gives the Apostle confidence that the Lord will continue to watch over him and bring him to 'His heavenly kingdom' (18).

Meditation: 'Luke alone is with me'—the earthly friend. 'The Lord stood by me'—the divine Companion.

Titus 1.1-4 God Never Lies

We have already seen in both the letters to Timothy how Paul delights to take the conventional epistolary opening and make that the means of bringing out important Christian teaching. He does it again here, with an emphasis on the reliability of God. God never lies and thus we may and must believe Him implicitly.

But as the convention demanded, Paul begins with himself. Nowhere else does he describe himself as 'a servant of God', though he does use the phrase 'a servant of Jesus Christ' (Rom 1.1, cf. Phil. 1.1). The following expression is far from straightforward. Literally it means something like 'according to the faith of God's elect . . .', which the RSV understands as 'to further the faith . . .' and the NEB, 'marked as such by faith and knowledge and hope— the faith of God's chosen people. . . .' The words appear to mean not so much the purpose or the mark of his apostleship as that it is this which is the very essence of it, the characteristic of it. His apostleship is grounded in and determined by the qualities named.

'The faith of God's elect' preserves a due balance between the divine initiative and the human response. 'Their knowledge of the truth' draws attention to the importance of apostleship in promoting advance in the knowledge of what God has revealed.

But the main part of this opening is concerned with 'eternal life'. This is spoken of as the object of hope. But this hope, as is usual in the N.T., is not a vague optimism, but the present conviction of something which is not yet but which surely will come. There is, of course, a sense in which eternal life is the Christian's present possession. But there is another sense in which its full realization is yet future, and it is this which is before us here. Though we do not yet see it, there is no doubt about it, for it rests on the promise of God and God 'never lies' (2). The promise goes back 'ages ago'. The manifestation is up to date, in the preaching of the Word as it has been entrusted to Paul. There may possibly be a glance at Jesus as the Word (as in John 1.1), but this is not the main thought. That is rather that God is pleased to manifest Himself in the preaching

27

He commits to His apostle Paul. Notice that Titus, like Timothy (1 Tim. 1.2), was a convert of Paul's (4).

Meditation: 'The truth which accords with godliness' (1). The truth of God is not intended merely to be admired, or apprehended, or approved; it is meant to be translated into action.

Titus 1.5-16 God's Stewards

Clearly Titus was a man of ability and one in whom Paul placed a good deal of trust. He had left him in Crete, he says, 'that you might amend what was defective' (5). This is a fairly tall order, but Paul appears confident that Titus would be successful. In the present passage Paul's concern is chiefly with the ministry. First he speaks of the qualifications to be looked for, and then of the opposite kind of teaching ministers would meet.

Paul says much the same to Titus as he said to Timothy on the qualifications required in ministers (1 Tim. 3). He speaks first of 'elders' and then of 'a bishop,' but this should not be understood in the sense that there were many elders in a church and but one bishop. As Barrett puts it, 'The elders you appoint must have certain qualifications, for a man who exercises oversight must be. . . .' Paul insists on the necessity of an upright life, a good home and family, and a firm hold on sound doctrine so that he can deal with false teachers (9).

Interestingly, the men of Crete were troubled by teaching with a Jewish flavour (10,14). Apparently it had something to do with food laws, for Paul cites a Cretan poet among other things for the expression, 'lazy gluttons'. But the main thrust of the quotation is that the Cretans 'are always liars'. This incidentally is written into the Greek language with the verb *cretizo*, 'to lie'. The poet also speaks of Cretans as 'evil beasts' ('vicious brutes', NEB). It adds up to a grim situation where very firm action is necessary. So he calls on Titus to 'rebuke them sharply' (13). There are occasions when the servant of God must take a very strong line. These people were thoroughly corrupt (15 f.). They required the firmest of firm hands.

Notes: V. 10: The worst heretics were Jewish, but these were not the only ones. V. 12: The poet is Epimenides (6th–5th century B.C.), though some think Paul takes the quotation immediately from Callimachus (3rd century B.C.). Epimenides was widely held to be a prophet and Paul evidently uses the general title. V. 16: This is surely the ultimate condemnation of the merely professing Christian.

Questions: (1) What other Scriptures than v. 16 distinguish between words and works? (2) How far does this fit your life?

28

Once again we have an emphasis on sound doctrine. Whatever be
the case with the false teachers Titus is to teach what is correct.
Throughout the Pastorals this concern for teaching what is right
is constant. But it is also the case that these same Epistles stress
the importance of lives that commend the sound doctrine that is
taught. Paul insists that right teaching and right living must go
together. At the end of the passage under consideration he urges
slaves so to live that 'in everything they may adorn the doctrine of
God our Saviour' (10), and this might well be held to apply to all.
Paul looks for Christians who will show by their lives what manner
of faith it is that they profess. As in *1 Timothy* he has instructions
for various classes in the church. The older men, who were in that
distant age looked up to as leaders and revered for their experience
and wisdom, are to show a due appreciation of the seriousness of
life (2). The older women are likewise to act becomingly and to
train up the younger. The injunction tells us a good deal about both
age groups. The younger women are to be specially careful of
their home and family duties (4 f.). It is, of course, still the case
that the effectiveness of their husbands' work and the future of their
children depend to a large degree on their making the home what
it should be. When he gets to young men, Paul singles out the
importance of self-control, an exhortation far from being out of
date in view of the undisciplined lives common in some quarters.
Titus himself is not excluded, and indeed the exhortation to him
personally is much more detailed than that for young men in
general (7 f.). To whom much is given of him shall much be required.
As elsewhere in the N.T. slaves get a special mention. As we saw
when dealing with 1 Tim. 6.1 f., Christian slaves, especially if their
masters were also Christian, were strongly tempted to presume on
their relationship, and Paul is very anxious that they should commend
the Christian faith.   *Notes:* V. 2: Notice 'love'; Paul always sees
it as important. V. 3: 'reverent' has a meaning like 'suited to a
sacred character'. For the Christian all of life is sacred.

Titus 2.11-15   The Grace of God

Having dealt with the kind of conduct he looks for in believers
Paul goes back to the basis of it all. The 'For' which introduces
v. 11 should not be overlooked. Men should live in the way outlined
because God has acted for salvation. 'The grace of God' is viewed
dynamically. It 'appeared'. In Christ the very grace of God was
seen. Grace is one of the great Pauline words (Paul uses it 100

times out of 155 times in the N.T.), and it emphasizes the freeness of God's gift of salvation. This is universal in its scope (Lock sees 'all men' as meaning 'all classes of men, even slaves'). It is in keeping with the characteristic emphasis of these Epistles that this grace 'trains us' in right living (12), and that both negatively and positively. It is reinforced by an appeal to the 'blessed hope,' the second coming of our Lord Jesus. This is distinguished from the first advent by the explicit reference to His 'glory'. Notice that Jesus is expressly called 'God'. The deity of our Saviour meant a good deal to the men of the N.T. and those moderns who have rejected the doctrine have cut themselves off from a considerable part of the riches of Christianity. It matters immensely that the salvation we proclaim is not one which proceeds from any created being but from none less than God Himself.

Christ's saving work is described in terms of redemption (14). This means the setting free from slavery or a death sentence by the payment of a price (called the 'ransom', cf. 1 Tim. 2.6). Here redemption is 'from all iniquity'. Left to ourselves we could not break free from our sins, but Christ's redemptive act frees us from both their consequences and their power. The result is 'a people of His own who are zealous for good deeds' (14). Nothing less is adequate as the fruits of our redemption.

This is a grand message. A grander has never been committed to men. So Paul confidently calls on Titus to proclaim it 'with all authority' (15). In this he speaks directly to the need of our day.

Notes: V. 13: Some favour the AV, 'the great God and our Saviour Jesus Christ', but this is not the most natural meaning of the Greek (there is but one article; 'appearing' is never used of God; 'God and Saviour' is a recognized combination). The RSV is better.

Titus 3.1-15   The Life of Faith

The duty of Christians to the State comes in for brief mention. They are to be submissive and obedient, for the State is performing a necessary function and one which would be impossible without the co-operation of citizens. In the same breath Paul mentions the necessity of being kind and courteous to all men (2). The believer has obligations to those who are outside the faith.

We should treat all men well, for we recall from what we ourselves were saved (3). In 2.11 Paul almost personified grace, and here God's goodness and loving kindness are treated similarly. They 'appeared'. That is to say they were made manifest, became visible in Jesus Christ. Paul proceeds to speak of our salvation through the mercy of God, a salvation which comes 'by the washing of regeneration and renewal in the Holy Spirit' (5). Most today see a reference to baptism. This is possible, though it is also possible that Paul is using 'washing' symbolically and defining it as regeneration and renewal. If a reference to baptism is held to be present it is not in the sense that the rite of itself conveys spiritual blessings, for in this context Paul is stressing the very opposite of ritualism. It is the activity of the Holy Spirit which is important. This is not to be separated from the work of Christ (6) but is its necessary completion. He goes on to speak of this salvation in terms of justification, grace, hope, and eternal life (7), a rich collection of significant terms.

Before he finishes Paul has yet another warning against false teachers (8–11). A significant feature of this section is the reference to repeated admonition (10). For a man to be rejected as a heretic there must be persistence in error in the face of repeated warnings.

Notes: V. 1: 'Remind them' shows that this is not a new instruction. They already knew it. V. 4: 'God our Saviour'; cf. 2.13. V. 5: 'the washing of regeneration and renewal in the Holy Spirit' is seen by some to be two operations (as NEB, 'the water of rebirth and the renewing power of the Holy Spirit'). The RSV is to be preferred. V. 14: To the end Paul insists on 'good deeds'.

Meditation: 'The saying is sure' (8). Collect and reflect upon these sure 'sayings' of the Pastoral Epistles (1 Tim 1.15; 3.1; 4.8,9; 2 Tim. 2.11; Tit. 3.8).

Questions for further study and discussion on 2 Timothy 3.10—Titus 3.15

1. Discuss the ways in which Scripture can profit modern man and train him in righteousness.
2. How should we apply the words 'be urgent in season and out of season' (2 Tim. 4.2) to our own situation?
3. What can we learn from the *Epistle to Titus* about the Person of our Lord Jesus Christ?
4. Gather the references to the attitude Titus should adopt towards the Cretans. How far are they applicable to our own situation?
5. How does Paul bring out the change made in men's lives when they are saved by Christ?

B

31

Philemon

This is a purely private letter from Paul to his friend Philemon about a runaway slave named Onesimus. It seems that Philemon lived at Colossae, and that this letter was sent to him at the same time as Paul's letter to the Colossian church (cf. the references to Onesimus, Col. 4.8 f., and Archippus, Col. 4.17). Paul was in prison somewhere (1), and he had evidently been the means of the conversion of Onesimus (10). Now he is sending the slave back to his owner, but this letter is evidence that he is taking every care to ensure that Onesimus be properly received. It is a delightful letter, giving us a revealing glimpse into first-century life and showing us from a new angle the way Christians lived out their faith.

Most scholars hold that the imprisonment in question was in Rome, and that it came toward the end of Paul's ministry. It is possible that it was during another of Paul's imprisonments (2 Cor. 11.23). There is no way of deciding the point.

Nothing is known of Onesimus other than what we learn here, though there was a tradition in the early Church that he became a bishop. Similarly, nothing is known of Philemon other than what we glean from this letter.

Philemon 1-7   Refreshing the Hearts of the Saints

Once again we have the typical beginning to a first-century letter. Paul characterizes himself by his current imprisonment, which he sees as 'for Christ Jesus'. He links Timothy with him in sending the letter, but there seems no reason for thinking that Timothy had any real part in its composition. The recipients are Philemon, Paul's 'beloved fellow worker', Apphia (apparently Philemon's wife) and Archippus (who may well have been the son of the house; a little message is sent to him in Col. 4.17). 'The church in your house' appears to mean that a local group of Christians assembled for worship in the home of Philemon. What relationship such a house church had to the church of the city we have no means of knowing.

Paul goes on to say that he gives thanks for his friends. It is characteristic that the two qualities he specially notes are love and faith (5). There is no substitute for love in living out the Christian life. And, of course, unless there is a genuine faith in Jesus Christ there is no Christian life at all. It is likely that we should link love with faith as directed towards Christ and all the saints (rather than thinking of this as referring to faith only). Paul goes on to speak of the way he himself had derived 'much joy and comfort' from the same love, and he explains that 'the hearts of the saints have been refreshed through you' (7). An outgoing love (which ought to be characteristic of the way all Christians live) has far-reaching effects. Obviously it makes an impression on its immediate objects. But it does not stop there. Philemon's kindnesses to the saints at large brought joy and comfort to Paul and doubtless to many others as well. And, though Paul does not mention it, such love has its effects on those outside the circle of believers. 'Behold, how these Christians love one another!' was a verdict which brought the heathen world to take seriously the faith that could produce such results. It may well be that many of the troubles besetting the contemporary Church would be solved or at least considerably lessened if the whole Church structure were permeated by a spirit of love.

But we must not go on from there to conclude that the Church's business is simply to show love. Paul commends Philemon for sharing his faith (6). There is no substitute for believing on the Lord Jesus Christ and we should be quite clear about this. It is only by faith that we may obtain 'all the good that is ours in Christ'.

Philemon 8-25   That Useful Man Onesimus

From this section of the letter we are able to gather what had happened. Onesimus had been a slave of Philemon's (16), but had run away, possibly robbing his master before he left (18). He did what many other escaping slaves did, and went to the big city where it would be almost impossible to find him. But somehow he had been brought into contact with Paul the prisoner and Paul had been the means of his conversion (10). Now questions arose: What is the place of a runaway slave who has become a Christian? What should be done about the fact that legally he is still the property of his owner?

Paul is clear on the matter. Onesimus must go back. He is a Christian, and a Christian respects the rights of others no matter at what inconvenience to himself. So Paul sends him back to his master. It must have been difficult for him but he does it. And it must have been difficult for Onesimus. After all he had made good his escape and was presumably safe from recapture. Voluntarily to go back to the slavery from which he had broken free could not have been easy, quite apart from the fact that he must face whatever penalties were involved in his having escaped in the first instance. He might feel that Philemon would not be hard on him, but he could not be sure. But he was a Christian. And that meant that he must do what was right even if it meant hardship.

This letter, then, is Paul's attempt to ensure that Onesimus is well treated when he returns. It has been held up as a model of tact, as the Apostle gently but persistently pleads for one who quite plainly had become very dear to him (12). He could command (8), but prefers that Philemon should act of his own free will (14). But he does remind his friend of what he owes to Paul (19), and of the value Onesimus the Christian would be to his master (16).

Paul makes something of the meaning of the name Onesimus, 'profitable' or 'useful.' Formerly this man had done anything but live up to his name. Now he is a valued helper of Paul's (13); he is 'the faithful and beloved brother' (Col. 4.9). So had Christ transformed this most unpromising piece of humanity.

Hebrews

INTRODUCTION

This writing is anonymous. The ascription to Paul is fairly early, but by no means early enough to be decisive, and the style of the Epistle is against it. It is very different from Paul's normal style. A number of possible authors have been suggested, such as Barnabas, Apollos, and Prisca. But these are no more than guesses and we must accept the fact of our ignorance.

The recipients of the writings have traditionally been seen as Jewish Christians, tempted to relapse into Judaism. In recent times this view has been challenged by scholars who maintain that there is no way of knowing whether the writing was meant for Jews or Gentiles. They point out that the appeal to the O.T. as sacred Scripture was accepted by Christian Gentiles as well as Jews, and that the author nowhere says that he is writing to Jews. This view cannot be ruled out as impossible. But it is to be doubted whether it explains those many parts of the writing which insist on the superiority of some aspect of Christianity to something Jewish. It still remains the most likely view that Jews are in mind. But it is not written to Jewish Christians as a whole. It is clear that the recipients are a small group who might have been expected to be teachers but who had not made the progress in the faith expected of them (5.12).

It is not easy to date the Epistle. Perhaps it is relevant that there is nothing in it which indicates that Jerusalem had fallen, for in view of the line of argument adopted we might well have anticipated a reference to that event if it had taken place. On the other hand, there has been time for the gospel to spread to some degree and a certain amount of development both of doctrine and Christian maturity are presupposed. Perhaps we will not be far wrong in dating it in the 60's.

We have spoken of the writing as an 'Epistle', but this may be going too far. It certainly does not have the normal epistolary framework and it reads more like a theological treatise than a letter. We may retain the name 'Epistle' owing to its long use. But we should bear in mind that it is not by any means an exact description of the writing's literary genre.

Hebrews 1.1-4   The Revelation of God

This little paragraph forms an introduction to the Epistle as a whole. It concentrates on the revelation God has made of Himself (do not overlook the implication that men of their own selves do

35

not come to know God). He has revealed Himself in many different ways from times of old, as the prophets witness (1). But the culmination of the revelation has been reserved until recent times when He spoke 'by a Son' (2). The contrast is between the prophet who knows God externally and can say only the things that are given him from outside, and the Son who shares in the nature of deity and can speak of what God is in Himself, and for that matter show what God is in His deeds as well as His words.

Our author proceeds to bring this out by insisting on the high place Christ occupies. 'Whom He appointed the heir of all things' (2) should not be understood as if God adopted Christ into His family. Rather it is a way of saying that Christ stands to God in the relation of heir. It is a way of emphasizing His excellence, not of bringing Him down to the level of created beings. Far from being Himself created He was the means of the world's creation. He 'reflects the glory of God and bears the very stamp of His nature'. He upholds the whole universe. He 'made purification' for men's sins. He sits at God's right hand. It is difficult to see how words could more clearly convey the thought that He belongs with God and not with man, that in Him we see the very revelation of God Himself.

Notes: V. 3: 'reflects' really represents a noun with a meaning like 'effulgence'; it is not so much that He reflects glory from elsewhere as that the divine glory shines from Him. 'Very stamp' (*character*) means exact representation. He shows us exactly what God is. 'When He had made' is an aorist tense which points to a completed work. This is brought out also with the reference to sitting at God's right hand.

Question: Is Christ in your affections?

Hebrews 1.5-14   Christ is Superior to Angels

The whole of the opening phase of the argument is directed towards showing the surpassing excellence of the Christ from whom the readers were tempted to fall away. First our author shows that He is far greater than the angels. His method is to assemble an interesting collection of passages from the O.T. which combine to prove his point. He cites Psa. 2.7 to show that God does not speak to any angel in the way He speaks to His Son. It is this Father–Son relationship which is seen also in 2 Sam. 7.14, originally spoken with reference to Solomon, but here interpreted of the Messiah, the very Son of God. Next we turn to the function of the angels, which is to worship God's Son and thus definitely to take the lower place (the quotation might be from the Septuagint of Deut. 32.43 or

Psa. 97.7). Psa. 104.4 follows with its definite placing of the angels in the category of 'winds' (or 'spirits') and among the 'servants'. In strong contrast Psa. 45.6 f. addresses the Son in terms of everlasting sovereignty. This puts Him outside the class of the angels. But it is significant that the quotation is continued in terms of moral uprightness. We miss the Son's true greatness if we concentrate on power and glory. His sceptre is a righteous one (8). His love is for righteousness (9). It is this which the psalmist sees as the reason for the Son's superior exaltation (9).

With this our author links Psa. 102.25–27, with which he combines an expression from Isa. 34.4. Again he uses the Septuagint, for the Hebrew does not contain the word 'Lord'. But the revealing thing is that he has taken words which in the original apply to Jehovah and has used them of Christ. This shows as nothing else could the very high place he assigns Him. The quotation sees the Son as having a part in creation and as remaining unchanged while the creation grows old. His eternity is not to be overlooked.

The final quotation is from Psa. 110.1, a passage which is often cited of Christ. The words speak of God as giving Him a place at His right hand (the place of highest honour), and as overcoming all His enemies. Over against all this the angels appear as no more than 'ministering spirits', and indeed spirits whose task is to serve for the sake of saved men (14). Clearly Christ is pre-eminent over them all.

Meditation: 'Salvation' (14), like 'eternal life', is at once present and future (Westcott).

Hebrews 2.1-4 So Great Salvation

The stature of the Saviour shows the quality of the salvation. Since Christians have a Saviour so infinitely superior to the highest of created beings they must regard the salvation He wrought for them as no common thing. It is a salvation to be prized highly and sought out diligently. Yet it is easy to miss it, for this requires not a deliberate rejection but simply a drifting away from it (1). 'We are all continuously exposed to the action of currents of opinion, habit, action, which tend to carry us away insensibly from the position which we ought to maintain' (Westcott). It is the case that we may fail to attain salvation simply by neglecting it (3). God has made ample provision for the needs of all men. But if we neglect the means He has provided for our deliverance, then indeed 'how shall we escape?'

The greatness of the salvation is brought out by a comparison of the Christ, who procured it, with the angels. Elsewhere in the N.T. we read that angels played a part in the giving of the Law on Mt. Sinai (Acts 7.53; Gal. 3.19). This is not mentioned in the O.T. but our writer sees it as a way of stressing the dignity and importance of the old Law. This Law (here called 'the message', Gr. *logos*) was fully established (RSV, 'valid') and every failure to keep it brought retribution. This opens up the way for the 'how much more?' type of argument of v. 3.

The Christian salvation is thoroughly attested. Appeal is made to three different witnesses to establish this. It was in the first instance 'declared' by Christ Himself. This will refer to His preaching, but also to His actions. He set it forth by what He said and was and did. Secondly, it was 'attested to us by those who heard Him' (3). That is to say, the recipients of this letter had good grounds for accepting it. The gospel had been preached to them by people who had heard Christ. And finally, God bore witness by unusual happenings which attended the preaching. The Holy Spirit had done wonderful things. The final 'according to His own will' (4) is a reminder that these miraculous happenings are not under men's control. God acts as it pleases Him, not as men may demand, a truth which is not yet out of date.

Thought: You need not do anything to drift!

Hebrews 2.5-9   'Jesus ... crowned with glory and honour'

The wonder of the salvation of which he has been speaking now causes our author to bring before us the further surprising truth that 'the world to come' of which he is speaking, that world which is relevant to the salvation in question, was not subjected to angels but, as vs. 6 ff. show, to man. God has for men in Christ this high destiny. The quotation from Psa. 8.4 ff. brings out the high dignity of man. The RSV renders in the Psalm 'Thou hast made him little less than God', which is a fair translation of the Hebrew. But *elohim* can also be used of created beings (e.g. Pss. 29.1; 82.1,6), so our author's translation can be defended. But in any case, however the Psalm be translated, his main point stands: God has provided for man a great destiny.

Now comes a quite different thought. From the fact that we do not yet see everything in subjection to man, as the Psalm prophesies, our author turns to what we do see. And what we see is Jesus. The human name draws attention to Jesus the man, and we may fairly reason that the writer sees in Him the fulfilment of the prophetic word. He is the Man made lower than the angels. But He is also the recipient of the highest honour because of what He did when made lower in this way. It was 'so that . . . He might taste death', and not death simply, but death for every man. Thus early in the Epistle is the point made that the death of Jesus is necessary if we are to be saved. Paul tells us that death is 'the wages of sin' (Rom. 6.23), and we cannot doubt that this is the thought here too. Since men's sin involved them in death Jesus came where men are and died their death.

'By the grace of God' stresses the freeness of it all. It implies that salvation could not be accomplished by man's own efforts. But where man could not prevail God's grace could and did. The death of Jesus then was not an accident, nor the result of the malice of His opponents simply. It was the out-working of the divine grace so that the salvation of men might be accomplished.

Hebrews 2.10-18   True Man for Man's Salvation

Life was not easy for the little group of discouraged believers to whom this Epistle was written. Almost certainly they faced the possibility of suffering for their Christianity and they must have wondered whether it was worth suffering for. Why not give the whole thing away and enter into peace?

For one reason, says our author, because Jesus suffered. And was this a dreadful accident that could not be guarded against? Not a bit of it. It was the way He saved men. To bring about our salvation He came where we are, even though this necessarily involved Him in cruel suffering and, in fact, death. But since men had sinned and brought the penalty of death upon themselves it was inevitable that their Saviour should enter their lot, and die their death. It was through death that He destroyed 'him who has the power of death, that is, the devil' (14).

To do this He had to become man. But this was the point of everything. His business on earth was not with angels. He did not come to save them (16). It was men who sinned. It was men who needed salvation. Therefore He became man and died and saved them. His genuine community of nature with us shows God's passionate concern that we be saved.

Our author speaks of Christ's being made 'perfect through suffering' (10). This does not, of course, mean that before suffering He was not perfect. But there are different kinds of perfection. The perfection of the bud is one thing and that of the flower another. There is a perfection involved in actually having suffered which

39

does not exist apart from the experience of having suffered. Christ does not merely love us enough to suffer for us. He loved us so much that He *did* suffer for us.

A series of quotations brings out His community of nature with us. These come from Psa. **22.**22 (where the key word is 'brethren'), Isa. **8.**17 (Septuagint; if He trusted in God He was certainly man), and Isa. **8.**18 ('the children'). The real humanity of Jesus was a necessity if He was to be our Saviour. Only by becoming man could He take man's death and remove man's condemnation. Our passage concludes with some other aspects of this saving work. Christ became 'a merciful and faithful high priest' (17). This concept is found in *Hebrews* only in the N.T., but, as this writing shows, it is a powerful way of bringing out what Christ has done for us. And arising out of this is the thought, full of solace to the tempted, that Christ can indeed help them, for He Himself knows suffering and temptation and that from experience (18).

Notes: V. 10: 'pioneer' (Gr. *archēgos*), like Eng. 'leader', can mean first along the way or first in importance, and in addition it can mean originator. Christ was all these. V. 17: 'to make expiation' is rather 'to make propitiation' (RV); it is the personal process of removing wrath and not the impersonal removal of sin that the word denotes.

Question: Have you ever thought of suffering as something that may make you more like Christ?

Hebrews 3.1-6   Christ Superior to Moses

Moses was revered throughout the Jewish nation as the really significant man in the history of the nation. He it was whom God had appointed to lead the nation out of its bondage in Egypt and bring it to the promised land. And he it was through whom God had given the law to His people. The great miracle of the Exodus, with the plagues in Egypt and the crossing of the Red Sea, followed by the wanderings in the wilderness, with God's providential care over His people, and Moses as the mediator of God's commands and the leader of the nation, all combined to leave Moses with such an aura as set him apart from all the great men that followed. He was incomparable. There never could be another Moses.

To say that Jesus was superior to Moses, then, was to put Him out of the class of ordinary men. If these words are indeed written to Jews it is difficult to see how the point of Jesus' excellence could have been made more strongly. This is brought out first by speaking of Him as 'the apostle (i.e. the sent one; God sent Him for our salvation) and high priest of our confession' (1). This puts Him in a unique place as regards the Christian way. Only one person could have such attributes assigned to Him. And in fulfilling His task He was faithful. This is not unique, for men have been and are faithful in their generation (the degree of His faithfulness was unique, but that is not to the point here, so it is not mentioned). Specifically, Moses was faithful. But here there is a difference. Moses was faithful as a servant is faithful, i.e. in a subordinate position. Jesus' faithfulness was that of a Son (5 f.). Moses' faithfulness pointed, indeed, beyond itself ('to testify to the things that were to be spoken later'). But this fuller meaning was realized in Christ. Moses was a faithful subordinate, but he was a subordinate. Christ was not. The point is further made with the illustration of the house (3 f.). Moses was faithful in the house, but there is One with a higher glory than that. The illustration passes over to the builder as more worthy than what he builds. God, being the builder of all, is worthy of highest honour. Christ shares this honour, for He has already been associated with God in the work of creation (1.2). There is yet another shift in the house illustration when believers are spoken of as the house (6). This is a high privilege. But notice the importance of perseverance.

Meditation: Consider Luke 16.10–12

Questions for further study and discussion on Philemon and Hebrews 1.1—3.6

1. Discuss the light shed by *Philemon* on the resolution of modern social problems.
2. What can we learn from *Philemon* about life in the early Church?
3. Discuss the way the *Epistle to the Hebrews* brings out the greatness of Christ.
4. What do we learn in this opening part of *Hebrews* about Christ's atoning work?
5. Discuss the importance of the real manhood of Christ.

Hebrews 3.7-11   Disobedience

It follows from what has been said that it is most important that due heed be given to the gospel. Failure to respond to God's gracious invitation will have calamitous consequences, precisely because it is God's gracious invitation, and because it concerns the salvation wrought out for men by none less than Christ. Our author drives home his point by an appeal to Psa. 95.7 ff. Notice that the Psalm is ascribed to the Holy Spirit, the writer preferring to draw attention to the divine origin of Scripture rather than to the human author through whom the message was mediated. The quotation follows the Septuagint in substituting 'the rebellion' and 'the day of testing' (8) for the place names given in the Hebrew.

The point of the quotation is that during the wilderness wanderings the people did not heed the voice of God. Throughout the forty years they persisted in hardening their hearts, in rebelling against God and in putting Him to the test (this means something like seeing how far they could go). But failure to obey God is never finally successful. The full weight of the divine punishment does not necessarily fall at once, but the sinner is deluded if he thinks he can escape. The psalmist stresses the fact that God is never passive in such a situation. He is 'provoked' by those sinners, He recognizes that they always go astray and that they have not known His ways. The consequence is that they must experience the divine wrath. That this is certain is emphasized by the reference to the divine oath, the oath that they will 'never enter My rest' (11). In the context this must refer to the Promised Land. But it will also have the deeper meaning of fellowship with God.

Life is a serious business and it is well for us to bear in mind that failure to heed God's voice carries inevitable consequences. These days we do not like the thought of 'the wrath of God' and many have decided that there is no such thing. Granted that it is possible to interpret it in too human a fashion, the term yet draws attention to a grim reality. If a man persists in sin he must ultimately experience the divine opposition and rejection. And that is a frightening prospect whether we call it the wrath of God or whether we prefer some softer name.

Hebrews 3.12-19   An Evil, Unbelieving Heart

Following on from the quotation from Psa. 95 we come to the application. This example from Scripture shows that God is no respecter of persons. Even the people for whom He had performed the miracles in Egypt and whom He had brought to the very borders of the Promised Land were not spared when they persisted in unbelief and sin. The 'evil, unbelieving heart' that was in them could not but produce evil consequences. So the readers of the Epistle are warned against such a heart. It will surely lead to a falling away from the living God (12). There is an interesting combination of the individual and the community. The exhortation is addressed to them all. But they are to take care lest there be 'in any of you' unbelief, they are to exhort 'one another' and that constantly ('every day'). The community of believers has a concern for its individual members. It is difficult to preserve the highest standards of conduct and purity of belief unless there is a concern throughout the whole membership for the good of the individual.

A warning about 'the deceitfulness of sin' follows (13). Sin always comes in an attractive guise. For the original readers of the Epistle it was apparently in that of being faithful to the glorious heritage of the past. There are circumstances when such an attitude is eminently praiseworthy. But there are also times when it means the betrayal of what is highest and best. Here it signifies going back from the living Christ to that which was dead and gone. The readers are warned that to share in Christ it is necessary to persevere (14). It is not very hard to make a profession of faith in Him. But to continue as His servant through the difficulties of life is another thing again. There is paradox here. 'We share' is a perfect tense, indicating permanence. But the writer immediately goes on to say, 'if only we hold. . . .' This paradox is to be found throughout the N.T. Our salvation is given. It is all of God. We should never lose sight of this. But this does not excuse us from the obligation to persevere, and the N.T. writings contain many exhortations to constancy.

In vs. 16–19 we return to the Israelites who perished. Those who rebelled in the wilderness were not heathen men, men who had no knowledge of God. They were men who came out from Egypt under Moses' leadership. They had had such signal examples of God's power before their eyes and still had perished. Nothing external, but only continuing faith sees final salvation.

Hebrews 4.1-13 God's Rest

We now take up an expression in the Psalm, 'They shall never enter My rest'. Actually this has probably been behind the argument for some time, but the writer now openly concentrates on it. As the people wandered through the wilderness the 'rest' stood for the end of their troubles when they entered their Promised Land. But there is a deeper meaning than merely the cessation from external hostilities. Our writer recalls that the Bible speaks of God as resting on the seventh day from His work of creation (4). This indicates that there is a blessed state in which God is, and into which God's people might come. But when God swears that certain people will never enter it, then obviously the entering has not yet been accomplished. It is not these people, but some others, who will enter.

But perhaps the words apply strictly to the entering of Israel into Canaan? This possibility is ruled out by the date of the Psalm. Long after Joshua's generation had entered Canaan it was recorded that God swore they would not enter His rest. Clearly the 'rest' in question was something other than the uncertain rest of living in Canaan. The true rest still remains for the people of God (9). It is explained as resting from our labours as God did from His. This refers to the work of salvation. It is not obtained by strenuous striving. It is a good gift of God. And we do not enter into it until we cease from our own ineffectual efforts to obtain it and rest quietly on the promises of God. It is only then that we are really found resting in and with God.

It is then important that we concentrate on this rest and do not fall away by the kind of disobedience that ruined the Exodus-generation of Israelites (11). This leads to the reflection that God's Word is not to be taken lightly. It is conceived dynamically. It is not a static thing waiting for us to handle it as we will. It is 'living and active' and it stands in judgement on us. It is sharper than a sword, for it penetrates to the innermost recesses of the human personality (12). Nothing is hid from God (13). It is impossible to bluff our way through. The Word is always adequate, always revealing. We stand before God as we are, stripped of all pretensions and shams. This is a solemn warning still.

Hebrews 4.14-16   A Great High Priest

In the ancient world priesthood was accepted as a necessary part of religion. Everywhere men took it for granted that the gods are too holy for ordinary men to approach them. Worshippers need the help of a professional religious man, someone who knows the way and can intercede on their behalf. So the priesthoods performed their function on a thousand altars, for sacrifice was as universal as priesthood. Indeed a primary function of the priest was to offer sacrifices (cf. 5.1). The priesthood of the O.T. meant that the idea was just as much at home in Israel as anywhere else. It was, of course, axiomatic that some priesthoods were more efficacious than others. Like those engaged in any branch of human endeavour, priests differed in expertise, in local knowledge and in other ways. Thus all priesthoods were not put on the same level.

Our author makes use of all this to bring out important aspects of the Person and the work of Christ. Each of the N.T. writers has his own way of doing this, and in *Hebrews* we have the profound concept that Jesus is our great High Priest. He is the One who offers the sacrifice that really puts away sin and brings men to God. This can be seen as a process of redemption, of reconciliation, of justification, and much more. Seen as the work of a Priest certain aspects are emphasized in a way they are not when other metaphors are used. As the Epistle proceeds these truths will be unfolded.

In the passage now before us two significant thoughts about Christ are stressed. The one is His greatness. He is not simply a priest at home in a particular earthly sanctuary. He has 'passed through the heavens' (14), something that can be said of no earthly priest. But this does not leave Him remote from us, for the second point to be stressed is His sympathy. He came right where we are, was tempted with the same things with which we are tempted, without sinning. This may mean that He kept Himself from sin, or it may mean that He does not know those temptations which arise out of having sinned (as we, alas, do). But the main point is His community with us. He knows what we go through. Knowing then what kind of High Priest we have, let us 'with confidence draw near to the throne of grace'.

Question: How far have I really shared my weakness with Christ?

Hebrews 5.1-11   Christ our High Priest

The thought of high priesthood is carried on. First we are reminded of the things that characterize earthly high priests (the high priests of the O.T. are chiefly in mind). The principal thing is the offering of sacrifice (1), but there is an important qualification before a priest can do this. He must himself experience the weakness of those on whose behalf he ministers (2). It is this that enables him to 'deal gently' with those who fail. Of course, in earthly priests this means moral weakness, too, and such priests must offer sacrifice for themselves as well as for others (3). Presently our writer will bring out the point that this is not the case with Jesus, but for the moment it is the community of nature, the ability to understand, that he stresses. To this he adds the necessity of the divine call (4). It is not possible to have an Aaronic high priest without these qualifications.

With Christ our author takes up the two points in the reverse order. Our Lord did not take the initiative in order to make Himself a high priest, but was called of God (5 f.). The first Scripture quoted to demonstrate the point does not however mention priesthood. We must bear in mind that it is our author's basic concepts which control his manner of speech, not strict conformity to the illustrations he is using. It matters to him immensely that Christ is God's

Son, so he reverts to a passage he has already used (1.5) to bring out once more that Christ stands to God in the relation of Son. We must never lose sight of the fact that Christ transcends all that is meant by 'priest'. He is God's Son, and that comes first. But to this is added a further quotation which does see Him as a priest, a priest 'after the order of Melchizedek' (Psa. 110.4, cf. Gen. 14.18). Though Christ's priesthood resembles the Aaronic in some respects, it is Melchizedek and not Aaron who gives the significant model.

Next our author turns to Christ's earthly experiences which show Him to be one with us. The 'loud cries and tears' (7) presumably refer to Gethsemane. They certainly show that He understands our weakness. He 'learned obedience', which must be taken in the sense of His being made perfect (2.10). The meaning is not that He was once disobedient and became obedient, but that there is a quality of obedience known only through actually undergoing the costly act of obedience. It was in this way that He procured salvation for His people (9).

Question: What light do these verses shed on the problem of suffering?

Hebrews 5.12—6.3   Spiritual Immaturity

It is this passage above all which gives us a glimpse of the spiritual state of those for whom this Epistle was originally written. The writer expected them to have been teachers (12), which indicates that they had been Christians for some time, and that they were people of some ability. But they had not made the most of their opportunities. The result was that they were still in the kindergarten stage. Our author uses a variety of metaphors to bring this out. He does not think that the teaching he is giving is necessarily obscure. But it is so to them since they have become 'dull of hearing' (11). 'Dull' is literally 'sluggish' (the word is so translated in 6.12). Since they were sluggish in hearing, the explanations tended to be difficult. Their position is further brought out by a comparison of the food used by the child with the 'solid food' of mature men. Milk is, of course, proper food. But it is proper only at a certain stage of development. If the physical body is to be built up to its full stature it must have the solid food it requires. The spiritual parallel is not difficult. The immature Christian lacks skill in the teachings about righteousness (which might mean righteousness of life, but more probably has to do with the righteousness that comes

46

by faith). By contrast, the mature have trained faculties and discern good from evil (14).

It is interesting to notice what our author counts as 'elementary doctrines' when he goes on to exhort friends to go forward in the faith (6.1). Repentance and faith come first, for they are basic. A man must repent of his evil ways and really have faith, else he is not a Christian at all. It seems that 'ablutions' is a way of referring to rites with water practised by religions in general. It is elementary that the Christian should know what his religion teaches about baptism in distinction from the lustrations practised by others. The laying on of hands may point to something like confirmation or ordination, or it may point to a general rite for separation to a particular work. We are handicapped by not knowing as much about the practice of the early Church as the recipients of the Epistle. Resurrection and judgement (2) are doctrines to be learned early, as being fundamental to the faith. All this is a foundation and a necessary one. But it does not represent the last word. There is more to Christianity than that. And like the recipients of the Epistle we should go on to them.

Thought: It is possible so to concentrate on the sinner as to hold back the saint.

Hebrews 6.4-8   The Horror of Apostasy

For many Christians this is one of the most difficult passages in the Epistle and indeed in all Scripture. They see it as coming in conflict with the eternal perseverance of the saints and they find it difficult to think that no matter what sin a man has committed God should refuse to receive him back.

We should notice first of all that the state described here comes short of the full Christian experience. The Greek rendered 'the word of God' (*theou rhema;* v. 5) does not elsewhere stand for the full gospel message. And quite a number of important, even essential, Christian teachings are missing. For example, nothing is said about love. Can a man be said to have a full Christian experience if he is not practising love, love to God and to his fellow man? The passage appears to be describing the experience of a man who has enough experience of Christianity to know what is meant by it and what its demands are and who in the light of this full knowledge rejects it. Perhaps Simon Magus is an example of the kind of thing that is in mind (Acts **8,** especially vs. 13,20 f.).

The biggest difficulty to many is, however, the suggestion that those who fall away cannot come back. It is not easy in the light of

N.T. teaching in general to hold that God will refuse any sinner who calls upon Him, no matter how grievously he has sinned. But that is not what this passage is saying. Rather, it says that when a man really understands and really rejects Christianity he puts himself beyond the possibility of real repentance. He hardens himself in his chosen way. The passage does not say that God will refuse him. It says he cannot repent. The present participles rendered 'since they crucify . . . and hold Him up to contempt' (6) are significant, for they point to continuing attitudes: 'There is an active, continuous hostility to Christ in the souls of such men' (Westcott). It is not an occasional sin of which our author writes but a persistent attitude. Some indeed suggest that we should translate 'while they crucify. . . .' (so RV margin). Whether we do or not our, author is not referring to a time when these men have ceased to crucify Christ by their manner of living.

But in our concern for such difficulties of interpretation we should not overlook the fact that the passage is giving us all a clear warning of the dangers of going back on the knowledge of Christ that we have. There should be progress in the faith. To slip back is disaster, as even nature teaches (7 f.).

Question: What is the basis of true Christian 'assurance'?

Hebrews 6.9-12   Encouragement to Perseverance

The last section contained a very stern warning. There is no mistaking the seriousness of the writer, nor the unpleasant nature of the fate that he sees awaiting the apostate. It is comforting now to come upon this section which makes it clear that, while he has found it necessary to give warning to his friends, his confidence is that they will not go back. He is sure of 'better things that belong to salvation' (9), i.e. there are things about the readers which connect them with salvation (the Greek is a little obscure, but this seems to be the sense of it).

The basic reason for this is the faithfulness of God. God is not unjust. He takes notice of the realities of the situation and included among these is the fact that our author's correspondents are manifesting the truly Christian quality of love. If men who call themselves Christians are manifesting a warm love to their fellow men then the inference is that God is at work in them. And the further inference is that they are not on the way to apostasy. The love spoken of was shown in the past and still continues. It is no ephemeral thing, but something which carries on, and this strengthens the conviction that these men are in fact right with God.

But the end is not yet. Further, the love shown by the group is not necessarily shown by each and every member of it, and it is this to which the writer now directs his attention. It is important that 'each one of you' persist in the right way. Merely to be members of a group who are on the whole doing the right thing is not enough. There is a necessary element of personal participation. In encouraging them to persevere right to the end the writer draws attention to the examples of those who had gone before. He warns against sluggishness, and looks for 'faith and patience', an interesting combination. There is the combination of a reliance on God and a readiness to endure. And it is in this way that they (and we) inherit the promises.

Hebrews 6.13-20   God's Promise is Sure

The thought of promise is continued. Believers are not seeking some paradise of their own creating. They are servants of a God who has made provision for their salvation and who holds out before them certain promises. It is important to realize that these promises are thoroughly reliable. If we put our trust in God we are not following some will-o'-the-wisp. We have entered on a path that cannot but lead to the goal.

We see this in the case of Abraham, to whom God made a promise which He confirmed with an oath (13). In due course Abraham obtained what God had promised, though not without exercising patient endurance (15). God swore to Abraham and He performed His oath.

Among men an oath is the ultimate way of confirming what they have to say (16). So when God wished to convey to men the unalterable character of His promise, His unswerving determination to do as He had said, He confirmed His promise with an oath. The oath in question appears to be the one already spoken of; that to Abraham. It is relevant to a wide circle, for it includes Abraham's descendants, and indeed 'all the families of the earth' (Gen. 22.17 f.; Acts 3.25). It is not impossible that there is a side glance at the oath mentioned in Psa.110.4 which concerns the priesthood of Christ and which our author will quote in 7.21. But the main thought here is that God's faithfulness to Abraham is an encouragement to believers still. Now they have 'two unchangeable things', the promise and the oath, on which to rely.

This leads to the thought of the hope set before us (18), that hope which is 'a sure and steadfast anchor of the soul' (19). Hope in the N.T. is not a vague optimism about the future. Rather it denotes something which is certain, though as yet unrealized. The certainty is one which is attained by faith, and there can be no other way of attaining it, else hope would not be hope. Our hope is one which reaches right out into that holy place where Jesus now is. That is to say, it gives us assurance that we will one day be where He is. And this will be not through any merit of our own, but because of the high priestly work He has performed on our behalf (20).

Thought: Hope, like the Anchor, is fixed on the Unseen.

Questions for further study and discussion on Hebrews 3.7—6.20

1. How does the concept of rest help our understanding of the Christian life?
2. In what respects does the concept of priesthood help us understand Christ's work for men?
3. What do you understand by the 'elementary doctrines' of the Christian faith?
4. How may we guard against a failure to persevere?
5. What can we learn from these chapters about the importance of (*a*) love, and (*b*) hope?

Hebrews 7.1-10   Melchizedek's Priesthood

Melchizedek, the king of Salem and a priest of God, comes before us only in one incident, that in which he met Abraham as the patriarch returned from the slaughter of certain kings. He brought him bread and wine and blessed him. Abraham gave him a tenth of the spoil (Gen. 14.17–20). There is one further reference to this mysterious figure, namely in the Psalm already quoted and to which our author will refer again, Psa. 110.4, 'You are a priest for ever after the order of Melchizedek.' And that is all. Jewish thinkers on the whole neglected Melchizedek. For them priesthood came from Aaron and any other was ignored.

But the great contribution the writer of *Hebrews* makes to our understanding of the meaning of priesthood is an unfolding of the significance of this priest-king. He finds many things about Melchizedek which help us to understand what Christ has done for us. He enumerates some of them here. The name Melchizedek means 'king of righteousness' and the title 'king of Salem', 'king of peace'. It is also the case that no genealogy of this man is listed, though priests were usually very careful about such matters. Nor is there recorded anything about his birth or death. All this gives a fine picture of a priest who 'has neither beginning of days nor end of life' (3). But notice that he is said to resemble the Son; it is not the

Son who resembles Melchizedek. In other words it is Christ's priesthood that is the standard, not that of Melchizedek. All that the latter does is to provide a useful illustration which brings out certain aspects of Christ's priesthood.

The greatness of Melchizedek next occupies attention (4–10). This is brought out mainly by the facts that Abraham paid tithes to Melchizedek and that he received the priest's blessing. The former fact helps us see that the Aaronic priesthood is inferior. Its progenitor, Levi, 'was still in the loins' of Abraham when the tithe was paid, and thus there is a sense in which Levi paid the tithe (and thus took up the place of inferiority). This is involved also in the blessing, for the less is blessed by the greater (7). All in all, Melchizedek has much to teach us about the kind of priesthood Christ exercised.

Meditation: V. 2. There can be no real peace without righteousness.

Hebrews 7.11-14   A Change of Priesthood

Another aspect of the subject of priesthood is implied in the very existence in Scripture of a reference to the priesthood after the order of Melchizedek. If the Aaronic priesthood had done all that was required, men's priestly needs would have been fully met. There would have been no need and no place for another priesthood. The reference in the Psalm should thus have made thinking Israelites realize that the Levitical priesthood was inadequate. It is not that that priesthood did nothing. Under it the people received the Law (11) which was a great good (and would have been a greater had they realized the true function of the Law and the way it could point them to Christ; cf. John 5.46 f.; Gal. 3.19,24).

But Psa. 110 does speak of a priesthood after the order of Melchizedek. It sees this as persisting for ever. This obviously means a change in priesthood. But it also means 'necessarily a change in the law as well' (12). The Law cannot remain unaffected when the Aaronic priesthood is replaced by another. The Law, and the priesthood which offered the sacrifices prescribed by the Law, are closely bound up together. The one cannot be done away with without serious modifications in the other. Paul can speak of Christ as 'the end of the law' (Rom. 10.4), and our writer is making the same essential point in his own way.

The particular point which receives stress is that our Lord came from a tribe which was never by the Law connected with priesthood. Judah is the royal tribe, and the fact that Jesus came of this tribe

51

accords with the fact that Melchizedek was king as well as priest. The new priesthood in Christ is a royal priesthood.

Question: What are the benefits we gain from the priesthood of Christ?

Hebrews 7.15-19 A Better Hope

The superiority of Christ's priesthood is before us again. It is not quite certain to what the 'This' which opens v. 15 refers, whether to the 'change in the law' (12) or the inferiority of the Aaronic priesthood. These are closely connected and perhaps we should not make too sharp a distinction. But it does seem that it is priesthood which is primarily in mind here.

The point of high importance that is singled out is that Christ's priesthood is 'not according to a legal requirement concerning bodily descent but by the power of an indestructible life' (16). Set thus in sharp contrast the constitutive principles of the two priesthoods show the marked inferiority of the Aaronic. It was, of course, the case that to be a priest of Aaron's line it was necessary only to be born into a particular family. And it is obvious that this confers no special efficacy on the priest so born. But with Christ it is different. It is the quality of His life that makes Him the kind of priest He is. The word translated 'indestructible' (*akatalutou*) is important. It signifies 'that cannot be dissolved' and not simply 'endless'. It is the quality of the life and not its duration that is in mind. The term is set in contrast 'bodily', which is more exactly 'fleshy', 'expressed in flesh'. That which cannot be dissolved is in the strongest contrast to that which is merely of flesh. There is also a contrast between 'legal requirement' and 'power'. We should not see these two priesthoods as on the whole similar. They are strikingly different and that in the essentials. The thought of the quality of life is reinforced with another quotation of Psa. 110.4, the important words on this occasion being 'for ever'. Christ's priesthood will never be superseded. There is that in its very nature which makes it the final priesthood.

The other point which is stressed here is the contrast between the ineffectiveness of Aaron's priests and the effectiveness of Christ's priestly work. The former line of priests and the law which went with them were set aside because they could not effect that to which they pointed. But Christ has brought us 'a better hope . . . through which we draw near to God' (19).

52

The idea of permanence in Christ's priesthood is tremendously important. In the last passage we saw that the quality of indissolubility that characterizes the life of Christ is the really significant thing. It is this which is the basis of His priesthood. It makes it what it is. Now we find that there are important consequences to be drawn from it. Just as earlier Abraham's position was secured by a divine oath so is it with this priesthood. The indissoluble life would make it permanent even if it stood alone. But it does not stand alone. There is a divine oath to support it, and again we are referred to Psa. 110, this time to the words which refer to God's having sworn 'Thou art a priest for ever'. Thus both from the inherent nature of the life and the oath which God has sworn this priesthood is perpetual. The Aaronic priesthood was in due time superseded. Christ's priesthood will never be superseded. And this makes the covenant which Jesus establishes 'a better covenant' (22). The covenant stands for the whole way of approach to God. That which was associated with Aaron involved the offering of animal sacrifices and it was hedged around with a variety of requirements laid on the worshipper. If he failed to perform these the sacrifices were of no avail. Later in this Epistle the point will be brought out that in any case animal sacrifices are of no avail for the saving of men. They cannot put away sin (10.4). The way of approach which Jesus makes possible is from every point of view a 'better' way.

But the one thing which is being hammered home at this point in the argument is the quality of permanence. Clearly a covenant which depended on priests who could not continue was inferior to one which featured a priest whose life is eternal. Our author goes on to notice that those priests were limited in their ministry because from time to time they died. Death has an inhibiting effect on a man's work! But Christ is in sharp contrast. His priesthood is permanent. He continues for ever (24). Therefore He is *always* able to save those who come to God through Him. His intercession for them never ceases (25). This does not mean that He is a suppliant, but rather that His very presence before the Father in His capacity as crucified, risen and ascended is in itself an intercession which never ceases.

Thought: V. 25. 'I have prayed for you' (Luke 22.32).

This part of the argument is rounded off with a little summary drawing attention to the principal points brought out by the Melchizedekian concept of priesthood. There are three sections.

In the first it is the personal qualities of Jesus that receive emphasis. Moffatt remarks that 'it is generally misleading to parse a rhapsody' but there is a sequence of thought here which is worth noticing. Jesus is 'holy', a positive word denoting the ethical perfection associated with God, which is further described with two negative terms (forming an alliteration in the Greek), 'blameless' and 'unstained'. Then 'separated from sinners' is explained as 'exalted above the heavens'. Our author has been at pains to show that Jesus came right where we sinners are and took upon Him the weakness of our mortal nature. But He offered one perfect sacrifice to deal with our sins and now He is 'separated' from all that that involves. It is a favourite thought in this Epistle that sin has been dealt with once and for all.

The thought moves on to the sacrifice Christ offered. There is a small problem about the daily offering of sacrifices attributed to the Aaronic high priests (27), for the principal sacrifice which the high priest (in distinction from other priests) offered was the Day of Atonement sacrifice. This was an annual not a daily offering, and it is this with which our author deals principally. But there was a daily need for cleansing, and there were daily sacrifices. The high priest, of course, might offer these, and in fact Jewish writers like Philo speak of the high priest as offering daily. The expression thus accords with the office as understood at the time. In any case the contrast is between the repeated offerings under the Aaronic system (daily or yearly, the principle is the same) and the offering of Christ 'once for all'. There is a perfection in His offering lacking in theirs.

Finally, there is a contrast between the high priests in their weakness and the Son 'made perfect for ever' (28). We have before had references both to the Law (12) and to the oath (20). Now we read that the oath 'came later than the law', which means that it was the definitive thing, replacing what went before it. There is also contrast between the weak nature of the priests (they were no more than sinful men) and the Son. His relationship to God was very different from theirs, and this is rammed home with the 'made perfect for ever'. He has suffered for sin and in this way accomplished what is permanent in its effects (for 'made perfect' see note on 2.10).

Thought: 'It is I; have no fear' (Matt. 14.27).

Hebrews 8.1-7 The Shadow and the Substance

Throughout the ancient world there turns up from time to time a distinction between what is real and fundamental, and what is merely a copy or shadow of the real. Plato's distinction between the ideal 'forms' which are in heaven, and the imperfect copies which are all we see on earth at best, is well known. Our author has some such idea which he brings out at intervals during the following chapters. It is not the Platonic distinction (though it may derive ultimately from it), and is probably more indebted to Exod. 25.40 (quoted in v. 5). But it would have a wide appeal. The point which our author is concerned to drive home is that in the Levitical priesthood and sacrifices we see something resembling true priesthood and sacrifices. But the true to which the shadows point are found in Christ alone.

As he begins to bring this out our author outlines the chief points in his argument so far. First, he insists that Christ's is the true priesthood because offered in 'the true tent' (2), 'the heavenly sanctuary' (5). The fact that if He were on earth He would have no priestly ministry (4) is not significant It is what happens in 'the heavenly sanctuary' which matters, and the service rendered in what is no more than 'a copy and shadow' of that sanctuary is of comparative unimportance. There is a clear warning here for those who were tempted to go back from the Priest in the true sanctuary to the priests in the copy of the true. And we should not overlook the fact in our eagerness to condemn the recipients of this letter that in our age as well as any other it is easy to prefer the shadow to the substance. 'Christians' can still go through the motions, but without getting to grips with the reality or really reckoning with the wholehearted demands Christ makes.

The final thought leads us into the new covenant which dominates the next couple of chapters. The point made here is that it is 'enacted on better promises' (6). It is a covenant of pure grace, with Christ's atoning sacrifice at its basis. It offers men the promise of full and free forgiveness. Could this have been given by the first covenant, our author reasons, there would have been no need for a second (7). The very existence of the second shows the inadequacy of the first.

Meditation: Christ serves though He reigns, and reigns in serving.

Hebrews 8.8-13 The New and the Old

One of the most perplexing problems to the student of the Bible revolves round the expression 'the new covenant'. The Bible teaches that God does not need to work by the method of trial and error, as though He had to try one covenant and when it did not work, substitute another. He sees the end perfectly from the beginning. Accordingly, when He makes a covenant, we expect it to be binding for eternity. Yet Scripture speaks clearly of a new covenant and our passage tells us unambiguously that the first is obsolete (13).

The answer appears to be that there is a sense in which any covenant God makes is unchanging and unchangeable. Nowhere in the Bible, for example, is there any indication that the covenant with Abraham is abrogated. It still stands. God's way is the way of grace and this is abundantly clear in the covenant with Abraham. It is implied, in fact, in the covenant with the people in Exod. 24 (cf. Exod. 19.4 where God's action in grace precedes anything the people do). But spontaneously the people offered to obey God (Exod. 24.3,7). Indeed, while the covenant is initiated by God's grace there is the clear implication that the people will live as the people of God (cf. Exod. 19.5 f.). Increasingly the people came to understand this in a legalistic way. And increasingly they failed to live up to their obligations to God.

Since then they were unable or unwilling (or both) to respond to the grace of God shown in the covenant, the promise of a new covenant is spelled out for us in Jer. 31.31 ff., quoted in today's passage. There is a sense in which this covenant is the same one. It is still the expression of God's grace. But there is also a sense in which it is radically new. It involves an action of the very Spirit of God within men (10). It involves their having a real and personal knowledge of God (11). And it involves their sins being really put away (12), something which happened and could happen only in Christ's atoning work. Since Christ has made all these things possible it is clear that any previous arrangement is out of date. The old is obsolete and ready to vanish (13).

Question: Can you quote any passage of St. Paul's in support of this chapter?

Questions for further study and discussion on Hebrews 7.1—8.13

1. In what respects does Melchizedek form a model for our understanding of the priesthood of Christ?
2. Discuss the meaning and implications of the 'change in the law' (7.12).
3. How does the quality of Christ's life (7.16, etc.) help us understand the effectiveness of His priesthood?
4. In what ways does the shadow-substance idea illuminate Christ's work for us?

5. What implications do you see behind the expression 'the new covenant'?

Hebrews 9.1-5 The Tabernacle Furniture

The main interest of the author was in what Christ had done for men. But he clearly loved and had a profound interest in the Jewish institutions which foreshadowed the work of Christ. In a way without parallel in the N.T. he now dwells on the place and the manner of worship under the old covenant. Though now superseded neither was without significance.

It might have been expected that he would speak of the Temple, which would have been much more familiar to the men of his day. But he prefers to concentrate on the Tabernacle which had been used in the wilderness in the formative days of Israel. The essentials were, of course, the same as those in the Temple, so not a great deal hinges on the choice. But there was something about that first Tabernacle set up under Moses which might be expected to make a special appeal to those who loved the old way of worship.

The first covenant, he says, 'had' its regulations and sanctuary. The past tense may point us back to the days of Moses when it was instituted, or, perhaps more probably, may spring from the conviction that it had now been superseded by Christ's saving work. He speaks of two tents, the first being the Holy Place, the second the Holy of Holies. The word he uses for 'the Holy Place' (*hagia*, 'holy things') does not appear to be used in this way elsewhere, but is quite intelligible. He goes on to refer to 'the second curtain' (the first would have been that at the entrance to the Holy Place). This screened the Holy of Holies, the furnishings of which are detailed. There is a difficulty about 'the golden altar of incense' (4). In the first instance the word rendered 'altar' might mean 'censer' and some understand it this way. But the RSV is almost certainly correct. The term can have this meaning and it is this that is required. In the second instance the altar of incense was not in the Holy of Holies, but in the Holy Place. It had to be, on account of the use to which it was put. But in fact our author does not say that it was 'in' the Holy of Holies at all. He speaks of the Holy of Holies as 'having' it, i.e. it belonged to the service of the Holy of Holies (cf. 1 Kings 6.22). The offering of incense was an integral part of the ceremony of entrance into the Holy of Holies. The threefold reference to gold (4) stresses the glory of Tabernacle, as in another way do the references to the cherubim and to the mercy seat (5).

Clearly the old way had its values, even though not the ones attributed to it by the Jews of his day.

Question: How far is it right to deduce Christian doctrine from the design and furnishing of the Tabernacle?

Hebrews 9.6-10   The Tabernacle Worship

From the furnishings of the Tabernacle we turn to the nature of the worship that was carried on in it. While he notices the daily worship performed by the priests (6), our author's real interest is in the ceremonies on the Day of Atonement. He stresses the limitations on access to the Holy of Holies. Ordinary priests could never enter, and even the High Priest 'but once a year' (7). Nor did he have the right to enter as he pleased on that day. He must first offer 'blood' both for himself and the people. Our author does not see this as merely a piece of antiquarian ritual. It has meaning. It is unthinkable that God would bring about the setting up of a complete system of worship like this without there being profound meaning in what is thus established. In subsequent chapters a number of points in this meaning will be unfolded. Here our author's concern is with the fact that the careful hedging about of approach to the Holy of Holies is in itself significant. It showed that the way into the very presence of God was not open to sinful man. The people had no way into it. The priests had no way into it. The High Priest had no way into it for every day of the year except one. And on that one day his access was severely restricted. Could it be more plainly shown that the way to God was not open? Incidentally this is a truth which still needs to be learned. In our democratic days we are apt to take it for granted that we have the right to approach God whenever we will. The meaning of the Tabernacle furniture has an important message still.

The readers of the Epistle are reminded in conclusion that the ritual regulations were concerned with the purely external. They could deal with the body (10), but they could not deal with the problems of conscience (9). Ritual is not unimportant and it has lessons to teach us. But it has in-built limitations. It should never be regarded as effecting that to which it can do no more than point.

Meditation: How much better is the Christian Order, brought in at the 'time of reformation' (10)! Its institutions are spiritual, and its blessings universal.

From the ineffective our author turns to the effective, from the ritual to that to which the ritual points. He reminds us of the character in which Christ appears, 'a high priest of the good things that have come' (or 'to come'; the manuscripts are divided). Some understand 'the greater and more perfect tent' to be an imaginative description of Christ as passing through a heavenly sanctuary on the way to the Holy of Holies where He would perform His priestly duties, others see it as a symbolic description of the incarnation. What is most important is not the resolution of such points but the shedding of the blood of Christ on which our author puts his stress. All else leads up to this. He has already made the point that there is no more than a limited and purely external purpose achieved by the performance of ritual (9 f.) and he repeats this (13).

But in contrast to any limited effect secured in such ways the perfect sacrifice of Christ is efficacious. It secures 'an eternal redemption' (12). Redemption in the ancient world signified release from such a plight as slavery or a sentence of death, and release by payment of a price. Christ then paid the price which secured the release of sinners from their slavery to sin (Rom. 7.14), from the sentence of death that hung over them (Rom. 6.23). And this release is not temporary but 'eternal'.

Next we have Christ's work viewed as the mediation of a new covenant. Once again there is the thought of eternal worth (15), this being linked to the redemption which deals with transgressions even under the first covenant. The old sacrifices could not really take away sin. But Christ's death can and does. The Greek word *diathēkē* means both 'covenant' and 'will', which is the point of vs. 16 f. Our author plays on the double meaning of the term to bring out his point that the death of Christ was necessary. Death brings a will into effect and the death of Christ brought the new covenant into effect, just as if it had been a will.

Hebrews 9.18-22   The Shedding of Blood

We move back in thought to the old covenant, that described in Exod. 24. Its establishment illustrates the principle that blood must be shed to effect a covenant, for Moses sprinkled blood when that covenant was brought into effect. Our author gives us some information not found in Exod. 24, for example, the mention of the offering of goats, and the use of water, scarlet wool, and hyssop, and the sprinkling of the blood. In *Exodus* we are simply told that

Moses threw half the blood against the altar and half on the people (24.6,8).

Our author also goes beyond the O.T. when he speaks of Moses as sprinkling with blood the Tabernacle and the vessels used in worship (21; the historian Josephus also gives this information). This of course refers to a later event, for the Tabernacle did not exist when the covenant was made. In Exod. 40.9 ff. Moses was commanded to anoint the Tabernacle and its furniture, and presumably he obeyed this command. Nothing is said, however, about any use of blood at this time.

From this our author moves to the thought that the Law prescribed the shedding of blood on a number of occasions. Practically everything 'is purified with blood' (22). An occasional exception is allowed (cf. Lev. 5.11), but this merely highlights the rule. The teaching of the Levitical law is plainly that 'without the shedding of blood there is no forgiveness of sins' (22). Among many of the peoples of antiquity sin was taken very lightly and regarded as of little consequence. Nobody who took the sacrificial system of ancient Israel with full seriousness could make that mistake. The solemn ritual underlined two points: the seriousness of sin, and the necessity for the offering of a pure victim if sin is to be forgiven. In this way the people of God were prepared for the coming of Him who would offer the one sacrifice that really takes away sin. The sacrifices could not remove sin, but they had an important educational function. In the modern world where the pagan view of sin is so widespread there is still the need to learn the seriousness of sin and the necessity for the shedding of blood if it is to be put away.

Meditation: E'er since, by faith, I saw the stream
Thy flowing wounds supply,
Redeeming love has been my theme,
And shall be till I die. (Wm. Cowper).

Hebrews 9.23-28   The Perfect Sacrifice

Again we have the shadow and substance concept, this time to drive home the point that Christ has offered the perfect sacrifice. The sacrifices of the Law were of limited efficacy (13; cf. 10.1,4). They could 'purify' the 'copies of the heavenly things' (23) which is all that an earthly sanctuary can provide at best. But we need more than this if our eternal need is to be met. And that need has been met, because Christ has provided the sacrifice that perfectly meets our need. The writer sees Him as doing perfectly all that the ancient ritual foreshadowed. Thus the Holy of Holies, which was hedged about with such elaborate safeguards, and into which the high priest might enter and he alone, once only in a year, is no more than a 'sanctuary made with hands, a copy of the true one' (24). That which to the Jews appeared the very place of manifestation of the divine presence is now seen to be no more than a pointer to what really is true. But Christ ministers where it counts. He appears in God's presence for us (24). Our sin is dealt with at the highest level.

The second point that is stressed is the uniqueness of Christ's sacrifice. Our author comes back several times to the thought that the continuing nature of the ministry of the high priest is itself evidence of its ineffectiveness. But Christ did not offer Himself repeatedly. He made but one sacrifice. He offered Himself once for all (26). Intertwined on this occasion is the other thought that He offers His own blood. There is a quality about His sacrifice that could not possibly be seen in any other. The high priest necessarily entered the Holy of Holies with the blood of an animal, 'blood not his own' (25). There is a qualitative difference when Christ offers Himself.

The chapter concludes with a forward look. This must always be taken with seriousness, knowing that before all men is death and then judgement. Judgement is as certain as death. Indeed judgement is more certain than death, for some will still be alive at the end of the age and will be changed, not die (1 Cor. 15.51). But all will stand before Christ's judgement seat (2 Cor. 5.10). We should never take death other than very seriously. Yet the really important thing is not this. It is that when Christ appears again it will be for the consummation of salvation. Then He will not deal with sin but take His own into salvation. It will be a fearful thing not to be ready for Him when He comes.

Hebrews 10.1-10   The Will of God

There is a sense in which in this passage we come to the heart of the whole matter. Some misinterpret it by a wrong insistence on the doing of the will of God. They point out that our author quotes Psa. 40.6-8 in bringing out the truth that God does not delight in animal sacrifices. Prophetically the Psalm goes on to speak of Messiah as doing the will of God. Christ, then, the reasoning goes, has come, not like brute beasts who have no say in their being offered, but as man to make a perfect surrender of His will to God. The essence of His offering is the offering of a will completely subservient to that of the Father. In a day when many find sacrifice and substitution unacceptable such a view of the Psalm, of the teaching of this Epistle and of the nature of the atonement, finds many supporters.

But it is not what our author is saying. It overlooks his express declaration that 'by that will we have been sanctified through the offering of the body of Jesus Christ once for all' (10). Christ does indeed do the will of God. But that will is not expressed in vague generalities. It is the offering of Christ's body that is the will of God.

Our author introduces the thought by repeating that the sacrifices of the old covenant are ineffective (1–4). The Law has but the shadow, not the substance. It offers the very same sacrifices over and over in mute testimony to the fact that they cannot really cleanse (1 f.). They remind of sin each year (the Day of Atonement sacrifices are clearly in mind). But it is quite impossible for them to take away sins. Verse 4 is the definitive statement of the ineffectiveness of all animal sacrifices. Animals move on a different level from men. Their worth is infinitely less. They cannot possibly be accepted on behalf of men. It is this that makes the Psalm applicable. It categorically rejects animal sacrifices as the way, and puts the will of God in the supreme place. This means the abolition of the old way altogether and the substitution of something altogether new (9). The offering of the body of Christ is the one prevailing sacrifice. It is that which brings about the sanctification of believers. And our passage finishes with the characteristic 'once for all'. There is an air of finality about this sacrifice. It cannot be repeated. Nothing can be added to its perfection.

Thought: 'Present your bodies a living sacrifice . . . which is your spiritual worship' (Rom. 12.1).

Hebrews 10.11-18 Once for All

On a number of occasions our author has insisted that Christ suffered once and for all, and this is the central point in the passage we now study. Once again we are reminded that the Levitical priests offered repeatedly and that their sacrifices were totally unable to deal with sin (11). In contrast, Christ offered 'for all time a single sacrifice for sins' (12). Since His sacrifice really deals with sins there is no need and no place for a repetition.

The same point is brought out in a different way when our author speaks of Christ as sitting down at God's right hand. This imagery is repeated a number of times in the N.T. It is, of course, a metaphor, for we cannot conceive of spirits as having literal right hands or of adopting a sitting posture. But the meaning of the metaphor is important. Sitting is the posture of rest. It indicates that the One sitting has completed His work. That Christ is seated means that the work of salvation is accomplished. Nothing can be added to its perfection. That He is at the right hand of God means that He is in the place of highest honour. No longer is He despised and rejected of men. He is in the chief place in all of heaven.

Our author's interest in forgiveness is seen in the way he quotes Jer. 31. In ch. 8 he has quoted fully. Now he has the opening words about the new covenant, but omits a considerable section as he goes straight on to those about forgiveness. The new covenant is that which really brings forgiveness. The same point is brought out in another way when he speaks of Christ as having 'perfected for all time those who are sanctified' (14). The sanctified are those set apart for God by Christ's one offering. They are perfected because their sins are put away and they see them no more. This is for all time, for nothing more is needed. And we come back to this thought at the end with the reminder that where sins are forgiven there is no more offering for sin (18). Nothing can be added to perfection.

Hebrews 10.19-25   A True Heart

From the Saviour attention is turned to the saved. Since Christ has done so much for us there must be consequences in our attitude both to God and to men. Godwards the believer should have confidence. Because of what Christ has done for him the way into the very holiest is open to him. The curtain was rent in literal fashion to make open the way into the Holiest (Mark 15.38). And in a metaphorical way what had to be rent to make open that way was the flesh of Christ. The expression is poetic and vivid. Some prefer to take 'His flesh' rather with 'way'. The way through the curtain was His flesh, His human nature with all that this means. But the interpretation of the rending of His flesh seems more in accordance with the reference to His blood (19). What is clear is that we are being reminded of the access into the very presence of God which Christ's death brought to sinners, and we are exhorted to make the utmost use of that access. We should come with true heart, with faith, with assurance, and with our hearts purified inwardly just as water (the water of baptism) cleans our bodies outwardly (22).

For those tempted to go back there is point in the exhortation to hold fast and not to waver (23), as also in the reminder of what is involved in 'confession' and 'hope'. They should not try to stand on their own. Basic is the faithfulness of Him 'who promised'. God will not go back on His promises.

Believers can help one another. They can stir one another up to produce deeds of love and other good works. Notice how love is thought of as the most important thing in keeping men steadfast in the Christian life. And the assembling of Christians together is something not to be neglected (25). The assembly for worship, when all criticisms have been allowed their full weight, is still a source of strength to those who come with a true heart.

Questions for further study and discussion on Hebrews 9.1—10.25
1. What values do you see in the ritual and furnishings of the Tabernacle?
2. How does the concept of 'the new covenant' help our understanding of the Christian way?
3. Gather the references to Christ's sacrifice as being 'once for all'. What implications do these have for our understanding of the faith today?
4. Discuss our author's use of 'the blood'.
5. How does our understanding of Christ's sacrifice affect our daily living?

Hebrews 10.26-31 A Fearful Thing

We return now to the thought of the danger of apostasy. In mind is the man who has come to understand what the truth is, but who nevertheless has chosen to sin deliberately (26). He has rejected Christ, profaned the covenant blood and insulted the Holy Spirit (29). It is idle for this man to think that there stands before him anything other than certain and fearful judgement.

It is one of the besetting heresies of our day that this truth is not only rejected but regarded as sub-Christian. Men have so well learned the truth that 'God is love' that they have forgotten complementary truths like 'God is light' (1 John 1.5) and 'our God is a consuming fire' (Heb. 12.29). In the process they have distorted even that to which they hold, for they have confused love and sentimentality. The God of modern man is a morally flabby god, a little god who does not greatly mind if his worshippers go astray.

But the God of the Bible is a great God and One who loves, really loves, His people. He is infinitely concerned for their welfare and hates everything that makes them less than the best that they can be. True love opposes every evil in the beloved. It is this which is in mind throughout our passage when the writer speaks in terms of 'a fearful prospect of judgement', of 'a fury of fire' (27), and of what 'a fearful thing' (31) it is to fall into the hands of the living God. The fact is that we are not irresponsible children playing at life. We are responsible men, given each of us one life to live. We are to live it as those who will one day be called upon to give account of themselves. This is not meant to strike terror into us, but we are fools and more unless we see that life is too serious a business for trifling. Flippancy will not be enough when we stand before God and give an account of what we have done with His good gift.

Hebrews 10.32-39 A Call to Persevere

This passage yields a glimpse of the kind of trouble into which the early Christians constantly fell, all the more revealing in that it is incidental. Our author is not setting out to detail the troubles which Christians might be expected to face. He is exhorting his friends to remain constant in their adherence to Jesus Christ. In the process he reminds them of what they have already endured for Christ, and suggests that they should not let all this be in vain. Being a Christian in those days meant no token pain, but 'a hard struggle with sufferings' (32). It meant public abuse and it meant being linked with others so abused (33). It meant forfeiture of goods (34). There are Christians in modern times, as there have been in every age, who have such hardships to endure. Those of us whose sufferings are comparatively minor should have a lively sense of gratitude to Him who has shielded us from the worst. And when we do suffer, as suffer we must in some way, we should regard this as being in the true apostolic succession.

But our author is not dwelling on the sufferings of his friends. He recalls them, but he does not stress them. Rather his emphasis is on their being constant in their service of God. 'Do not throw away your confidence', he says (35). The implication is that confidence will normally remain. It is a wilful thing to discard it. Since God has done such a wonderful thing in us when He brought us salvation we have every reason for being confident. And we will remain so unless we give way to evil. For our confidence is not in any thing that we ourselves do, but in what God has done and will do. This does not mean that life is ever easy for the Christian. He must not expect that God will smooth out all his difficulties. That is not the path God's servants must tread. But if we cannot expect a smooth path we can expect help to get us over the difficult places. So our author exhorts to constancy. He recognizes that there are those who shrink back (38). But he does not think that his readers are included in the number. He links them with himself in the fine affirmation of v. 39.

Question: Can you imagine v. 34 being said of you?

Hebrews 11.1-7   Faith

The linkage of faith and constancy at the end of our last passage leads the writer to a more extended treatment of the subject. He begins by speaking of faith as 'the assurance of things hoped for' where 'assurance' translates *hypostasis*, 'that which stands under', and thus is the 'essence' or perhaps 'basis'. He is saying that faith is all that we now have of the things yet to be. It is faith that gives reality to those things (though not in the sense of creating them; faith simply apprehends them; cf. NEB, 'Faith gives substance to our hopes'). So with the following, 'the conviction of things not seen'. We do not yet see the realities to come. But by faith we know that they will come. It is faith which gives us the conviction of their certainty.

Faith is thus a very important quality for Christians. Without it they lack spiritual perception. With it they enter in some measure into an apprehension of what God has done and will do. The chapter goes on to bring this out, with illustrations from the lives of some of God's outstanding servants. First our writer deals with the theme in a general way. It was by faith that the ancients received God's approval (2). It was by faith that he and the men of his day recognized that creation had taken place and that 'what is seen' is not the last word (3), a judgement which is far from being out of date.

Today's passage contains references to three specific personages. Abel's offering was preferred to that of Cain because it was offered in faith. Enoch's being 'taken up' to heaven was due to faith, which elicits the important comment that 'without faith it is impossible to please' God (6). A man cannot reason himself or work himself into a place of acceptance of and acceptance by God. That is always a matter of faith. And Noah's faith was a condemnation of the world of his day as he acted on his profound spiritual convictions. Faith always shows up unbelief for the shallow thing it is.

Questions: Does reason have any place in Christian experience? If so, what?

Hebrews 11.8-12   The Faith of Abraham

Throughout the N.T. Abraham is regarded as the prototype of faith. And faith, for him, was not a conventional piety. The point first brought out here is his willingness to act with nothing to go on but his faith in God. He knew himself called by God and he knew nothing else. He could not have justified to unbelieving men a journey which meant leaving his country, his kindred and his father's house (Gen. 12.1). But his faith in God was such that he acted on God's word. He did leave his home, his family, and indeed his whole way of life.

Nor was that the end of it. He had been promised the land of Canaan, but he lived in it not as possessor but as a visitor. Isaac and Jacob shared the promise with him, but they all lived in tents, obviously temporary dwellers in the land. But Abraham's vision was fixed, not on the things that any man could see, but on 'the city which has foundations, whose builder and maker is God' (10). It is still the case that faith does not fix its attention on the same things as does the world. It is of the essence of faith that it gives the prime place to the leading of God.

Others were associated with Abraham. We have already noticed that Isaac and Jacob are said to have shared in his life. So also did Sarah, who was able to conceive only 'by faith' (11). It is worth noticing that her initial reaction was anything but one of faith (Gen. 18.12 ff.). But God did not judge her by her worst moment (as He does not judge us by ours). Sarah's settled attitude was one of faith, not doubt. She trusted God and 'considered Him faithful' (11). Thus God honoured the faith of His servants, and from one man 'as good as dead' in time there descended a great nation (12).

Hebrews 11.13-22   The Faith of the Patriarchs

This passage divides into two sections, the first a general considera-tion of what is implied in the faith of the men spoken of, and a second in which individual patriarchs are mentioned. The outstanding character of the faith of people like those just mentioned is shown by the fact that to the very end of their lives they never did see the realization of the promises of God. This happened, of course, because these promises are bound up with the saving work of Christ. Until He came there could be no complete fulfilment of God's promises whatever partial anticipations might be granted the men of old. But if they did not see the fulfilment there was nothing wrong with their vision. They saw themselves for what they were, 'strangers and exiles on the earth' (13). Had their interest been in earthly possessions they would have been able to go back to the land from which they came (15). But their vision was fixed on something far better, on that spiritual possession that God had for them. They were giants in faith. And it is a wonderful thing that is said of them when our writer reports that 'God is not ashamed to be called their God' (16). It calls for heartsearching on our own account as to whether God could in any meaningful sense be called 'our' God. Would He be ashamed of being called the God of people like us?

When he gets down to cases our author thinks first of Abraham's readiness to offer up Isaac, that son in whom God had said the promises would be fulfilled. The patriarch trusted God, and trusted that God can even bring men back from the dead. Indeed, our author sees a figurative resurrection in the way Abraham received his son again. Again, Isaac looked forward to a future he would not see as he invoked blessing on Jacob and Esau. And Jacob and Joseph followed in the same way by looking forward in faith to what they knew God would bring to pass after their lives had ended. Thus each of the patriarchs sets us an example. They all trusted God against the present indications. And in each case their faith was vindicated.

> Truth: *Faith, mighty faith, the promise sees,*
> *And looks to that alone:*
> *Laughs at impossibilities,*
> *And cries 'It shall be done!'* (*C. Wesley*).

Hebrews 11.23-31   The Faith of Moses

Abraham and Moses were regarded as the two really great men in the early history of the people. So when our author cites them as his outstanding examples of faith he is making a strong appeal to all who revered Jewish institutions and personages. In the case of Moses, faith was manifested even in his babyhood, for his parents needed faith to defy the edict of Pharaoh (23).

The point which receives special stress is Moses' readiness to put up with ill-treatment which he could have avoided by deserting the divine call. He could have lived as a royal prince, 'the son of Pharaoh's daughter' (24). Instead he chose to be one of the despised nation of slaves. Faith gave him clarity of perspective so that he could estimate aright the true significance of both. It is not being realistic, but suffering from a distorted sense of values, when a man prefers the 'security' of worldly safety to the 'uncertainties' of faith in God. On the long view it is faith that matters, faith that emerges triumphant.

This is brought out by saying that Moses 'looked to the reward' (26). He understood what the reward was if he cast in his lot with Pharaoh and his court. And he understood what the reward was if he joined himself to 'the people of God'. In both cases the lasting spiritual result and the immediate material result were in sharp contrast. So Moses endured steadfastly the present trial, his faith assuring him that this was of no consequence alongside the greater evil of abandoning the life to which God had called him. So it was the vision of 'Him who is invisible' (27) that sustained him when he left Egypt, having chosen the wrath of the ruler instead of his favour. And it was faith again which guided his actions in instituting the Passover. He had nothing but faith to guide him in keeping that feast himself and in persuading his fellow Israelites to do the same. But that faith was vindicated, as was that of the people when they crossed the Red Sea and when they captured Jericho. It is interesting to see Rahab among those who showed faith, a faith which led her to welcome the spies (31). In each case faith was triumphantly vindicated.

Hebrews 11.32-40
The Triumph of Faith

Our author has not exhausted the catalogue of the heroes of faith. There are many more and he lists some of their names (32). But for lack of time he does not go into detail in their exploits. Instead he has a quick summary. First he speaks of the broad, general results achieved by the men of faith: they had success in conflict, success in the area of government, and the spiritual reward covenanted by God (33). They also experienced forms of personal deliverance. Some were saved from wild animals, others from fire (which may stand for physical forces in general), and others again from men who would have destroyed them (33 f.). The third group of successes rings the changes on human strength: they won it, they used it in war, and they triumphed with it by putting armies to flight (34).

We may wonder why women are singled out as receiving their dead by resurrection (35). But most raisings recorded in Scripture were in fact for women (e.g. 1 Kings 17.17 ff.; 2 Kings 4.17 ff.; Luke 7. 11 ff.; John 11; Acts 9. 36 ff.), so there is point in the comment. But in rejoicing over such victories we must not think that faith is always triumphant on the human level. Sometimes it must undergo hardship and even apparent defeat. That was the way of the cross, and the Christian is to follow in the steps of the Master. So we are told of those who suffered in a variety of ways, some accepting death well knowing that their faithfulness would have its effects in the resurrection (35). Some endured only insults, some accepted torture, some imprisonment, some destitution and the loss of homes and the like.

But the climax to all this comes with the surprising information that, giants of the faith though they were, and examples to believers as they continue to be, these 'did not receive what was promised' (39). This does not mean that God let them down in any way. It is our author's way of making the telling point that in the providence of God the consummation of the promises was not in the days of old, but would include his readers. God's plan is that all His people will be perfected together. Christ's saving act has consequences for the whole people of God.

Thought: 'Out of weakness . . . became mighty' (34).

Questions for further study and discussion on Hebrews 10.26—11.40

1. How may we relate the Epistle's teaching on perseverance to the modern situation?
2. What value do you see for your own situation in the way our author relates faith to the unseen world (11.1 ff.)?
3. Our author links Abel, Enoch, and Noah (11.4–7). What common pattern do you discern in the experiences of these three?
4. In what ways is Abraham a model for later believers?
5. How does the example of Moses speak to an age which emphasizes material culture?

Hebrews 12.1-3   Christ our Example

There is dispute as to whether we should understand the 'cloud of witnesses' (1) as witnessing us as we live out the Christian life, or whether they are witnesses to the truth of the things of God from whose example we can learn much as we serve our Lord. In favour of the latter view it is pointed out that the word for 'witnesses' (*martyrōn*) seems never to be used of mere spectators. It is characteristically applied to those who have witnessed for the faith, and in time came to be applied specifically to those who witnessed by a martyr's death. In favour of the former is 'we are surrounded', which is not naturally interpreted of our looking to them, all the more so since the writer immediately goes on to say that we should have our attention fastened on Jesus (2). Perhaps there is a bit of both meanings. On the one hand the heroes of the past watch to see how we acquit ourselves. But on the other they do not do this as mere spectators. They are those who have

70

borne witness in their day, as they look to us to do the same in ours.

But the important thing is that we have a race to run. We should therefore strip ourselves of everything which may hinder us (the distinction between 'weight' and 'sin' indicates that there are some things which, though not sins, the Christian should avoid, since they are hindrances to his Christian advance). And especially we should fix our gaze on Jesus. He is our perfect example and inspiration. He is the 'pioneer' (*archēgos* is connected with the root denoting 'first'; it may be first in time or first in importance; Jesus is both; He is the one who shows us the way and He is our leader as we seek to follow). He is also the 'perfecter'. He both initiates and brings to completion the faith by which we live.

Especially important is the cross. This is, of course, the way our salvation was wrought out. But it is also our supreme example. Christ accepted it despite all the shame it involved (2) and now is in the place of highest honour. When we are confronted with open hostility it is a strength to consider that we serve a Master who knows it exactly. For our salvation He put up with the worst that sinful men could do.

Hebrews 12.4-10   Sons receive Chastening

It is one of the facts of life that we do not like suffering. Nobody does. But it is also one of the facts of Christian life that suffering has been transformed by the sufferings of Christ. When we look at the cross we see that suffering can be meaningful, and that it can accomplish great good. No one who has experienced in his own soul the saving benefits of the sufferings of Christ can ever look on suffering in quite the same way again. This is not to say that we simply utter the words 'the cross' and all our problems concerning suffering vanish. They do not. But the cross means that they must be viewed in a new light. They cannot be seen now simply as misfortunes which a God who does not greatly care allows to afflict us. The cross shows us that God cares passionately for us and our best good. And since God is all-powerful He must see meaning in the sufferings that come to us. Otherwise He would not allow them to come. In a number of places in the N.T. various aspects of the problem of suffering are brought out.

Here the thought that is stressed is that the sufferings of the Christian are evidence of his status in the heavenly family. They mark him out as a son, as one for whom God cares, and cares enough to discipline. Many today thoughtlessly maintain that suffering is evidence that there is no God, or that if there is one, then He is a God who does not care about His people. Our writer draws exactly the opposite conclusion. After pointing out that his readers should not exaggerate the problem, for they had not yet suffered 'to the point of shedding your blood' (as Christ did), he goes on to the important point that sons are disciplined. A father may not worry overmuch about people with whom he has no close connection, but he is very concerned indeed for the son whom he loves. The very fact that God allows Christians to undergo trials is evidence that He is acting as a father and that He loves them. He treats them as sons and disciplines them for their profit (10). Their sufferings are evidence, not that He does not care for them, but that He does, not that He regards them as outsiders, but that He sees them as sons.

Hebrews 12.11-17   The Right Attitude to Suffering

Suffering, rightly endured, can be the means of great blessing, both to the sufferer and to those with whom he comes in contact. That was made plain in the last passage we studied. Nothing, it is true, can make it pleasant (11). But a right attitude can make it profitable. It is this with which our author proceeds to concern himself. He points to 'the peaceful fruit of righteousness', i.e. the fruit which consists in righteousness. Notice his adjective, for 'peaceful' is not a description which would spontaneously occur to most of us. But when discipline is accepted the soul is at peace. It is rid of the tensions and divisions which make life difficult for the undisciplined. It is at one with God. This is real peace.

Because of this the writer can exhort his readers to lift their drooping hands and strengthen their weak knees (12; cf. Isa. 35.3), a vivid picture of men who are not realizing their full potential. In language reminiscent of Prov. 4.26 he urges that they make the paths straight (i.e. take away awkward bends and roughnesses). The lame will then not be hurt but healed. It is easy to live in such a way as to neglect the needs of the spiritually lame, but the man who heeds the discipline God sends him will not make that mistake.

'Strive' is perhaps better 'pursue'. There is the thought of diligent and eager pursuit. This is directed towards peace, here 'peace with all men'. This follows naturally enough from that peace with God which we have just noticed (11). With this is linked 'the holiness without which no one will see the Lord'. This does not, of course, mean that men must by their own effort produce such qualities of character as fit them for the vision of God. Such an idea cannot be fitted into the N.T. Rather the writer is speaking of earnestness in living out the gospel. If a man does not yield himself to God in response to Christ's atoning act he will not see God. This is something to be sought after from the depths of one's being.

Our passage ends with the reminder that some have had a certain acquaintance with the things of God but have failed to profit thereby. It is the thought of 6.4 ff. in another form. If men nourish a 'root of bitterness' they will surely fail to obtain the blessing of God. Esau is the example of the kind of thing that is in mind. We learn here that, subsequent to his rejection of his birthright, he wanted back the blessing he had once treated so lightly. But his renunciation was a solemn act which could not be undone by tears.

Hebrews 12.18-24   The City of God

The seriousness of the issues involved is now brought out with a reminder of the inauguration of the old covenant. At Mount Sinai there were various fearful phenomena which are listed for us (18 f.). The people who heard it all entreated that they receive no more such messages (19), and even Moses, the man of God, could say, 'I tremble with fear' (21). It is clear that the scene was one of terrifying grandeur. It emphasized the truth that God is not to be taken lightly.

But the purpose of drawing attention to Mount Sinai is not that we may concentrate on the terrors. They are there, but in the background. The emphasis is rather on the graciousness which is the characteristic of the new covenant. Not Mount Sinai but Mount Zion is the place to which Christians have come, and this is described as 'the city of the living God, the heavenly Jerusalem' (22). There is grandeur about this concept (as is strikingly brought out in *Revelation*, for example). We see this in brief compass in the references to the angels, the inhabitants of heaven, and especially to God, now characterized as 'a judge who is God of all' (23). While our author is stressing the graciousness of the new covenant he does not lose sight of the fact that it includes elements of seriousness, and even severity. The issues involved are of deep and lasting consequence. When we preach the gospel we should not think that we are playing a kind of game in which it does not greatly matter who wins. We are offering men salvation from a lost eternity. And as every man must stand before the 'judge who is God of all', none can evade the challenge.

But the climax is reached in the reference to Jesus Christ (24). There is one reference to Him as the mediator of the new covenant, and one to His blood (which, as it brings blessing and cleansing, 'speaks more graciously' than that blood that pleaded for revenge, Gen. 4.10). But in this short compass our author has managed to pack a world of meaning about the graciousness of Christ. His way is a way of full salvation for us and that a salvation by free grace.

Hebrews 12.25-29   'Our God is a Consuming Fire'

The previous passage has put emphasis on the graciousness which characterizes the Christian approach. It centres on the atoning work of Christ who shed His blood that our sins might be put away completely. Salvation is thus a great and free reality. But this does not mean that we can regard the issues involved as unimportant. To reject the grace of God is to invite certain damnation.

The comparison has been made of Mount Zion and Mount Sinai (12.18-24). But this is not to be understood as though one God was responsible for the former arrangement and another for the latter. There is one God behind the O.T. and the N.T. We should not mistake His grace for weakness. Indeed, if it was a fearful thing to refuse the God who was manifested in the thunders of Sinai, it is, when we get to thinking seriously about it, a more solemn thing by far to refuse the God who speaks so graciously in Christ. Or, as our author puts it, as they did not escape who rejected the warning on earth much less will they who refuse Him who warns from heaven (25). God did indeed shake the earth at Sinai, but another shaking is envisaged, a final one, from the same God (26). This turns our attention to the importance of a sense of values. There are some things that can be shaken and destroyed and there are others which are permanent. They cannot be shaken. They will remain throughout the time of this world's existence and beyond. This is one of the things from this Epistle which need emphasis in the world of today. Men are apt to regard all human achievements as no more than relative and to go on from there to think not only that human grasp of the truth is relative, but that truth itself is relative. They deny the absolutes.

Perhaps Christians have sometimes been too prone to cling to things that are temporary and to confuse what is merely cultural with what is essential to the faith. But when full allowance has been made for that, it is still the case that there is 'a kingdom that cannot be shaken' (28). It is that with which we have to do. To reject what it stands for is calamitous, for God is implacably opposed to every evil thing. He is a consuming fire (29), a N.T. truth with enormous practical consequences.

Hebrews 13.1-6 Christian Service

The readers of the Epistle are now exhorted to fulfil some practical Christian duties. We should never be so taken up with intricate questions of the bearing of Christian truth on philosophical difficulties or on the social problems of the day that we neglect the duties that lie ready to our hands. So Christians are to manifest brotherly love. This incidentally was apparently a new virtue; the expression 'brotherly love' appears in pre-Christian times always to have been used in the literal sense of love within a family. To have such love for fellow believers is striking. And it is something which formed a potent weapon of evangelism in the early Church, for the heathen were immensely impressed when they had to confess, 'Behold how these Christians love one another!' Hospitality is another virtue to be stressed. It was important to the early Christians, for as they travelled in the service of the gospel they experienced difficulties in securing lodging places. Inns were expensive and often of dubious reputation. Hospitality in Christian homes was important.

Prisoners were usually badly treated, so that compassion towards them was not out of place. The attitude looked for here is an advance on hospitality. Strangers seek one out and bring the opportunity for hospitality, but prisoners must be sought out. Probably Christians in prison for the faith are primarily in mind. The readers are to remember them 'as though in prison with them', as in fact in due course they well might be. For the attitude which these readers in fact practised, cf. 10.34.

In a day of sexual laxity the Christian attitude to marriage stood out. Sex is a good gift of God, and it is to be used in the way God intends, not as a mere gratification of the lusts. For the Christian there must always be the two thoughts that (a) marriage is indeed an honourable estate, and sex something that can be exercised 'undefiled', but also that (b) a severe judgement of God is against the immoral (4).

The last vice our author mentions is the love of money, which can be a fruitful cause of all kinds of evil. But when a man resists the temptation and is content with God's provision he will rejoice in a well founded confidence (6). Where God is Lord and guard we need not fear what man can do.

Hebrews 13.7-16
Christ our Sin Offering

We are reminded that Christians have a duty to their leaders, a thought to which our author will return (17). The leaders' manner of life is to be imitated (7). Perhaps it is the consideration that even the manner of life of the best men is subject to change which leads to the abrupt introduction of the thought that Jesus Christ does not change (8). Look back or forward it makes no difference. He is always constant. 'Diverse and strange teachings' (9) might lead astray. But the constancy of our Lord is an encouragement to us to be constant in our place.

The main part of our passage is taken up with a consideration of Christ's work for us viewed from the aspect of the sin offering. The 'altar' (10) should not, of course, be misconstrued as though it referred to any material earthly object. It is a way of referring to Christ's sacrifice for us, and if any material object is in view it is the cross. The interesting thing about the subsequent reference to the sin offering is that the part singled out for mention is not the manipulation of blood or the burning on the altar or the like. It is the burning of the bodies of the victims 'outside the camp' (11). These bodies were so identified with sin that they could not be offered on the altar. They were simply thrown outside the city and burned. This is a vivid way of saying that Christ in His death became one with sinners and bore their sin (cf. 2 Cor. 5.21).

This is made the basis for an appeal to the readers to be ready likewise to go 'outside the camp', not, of course, in any sense that they might be doing an atoning act, but in the sense that they are identifying themselves with Jesus, even at the cost of breaking valued earthly ties. All the more is this the case in that Christians have their citizenship not in any earthly place but in heaven (cf. 11.16). They should in accordance with their calling offer up sacrifices, but sacrifices of a spiritual character (15 f.). In the light of what Christ has done there are no others we can offer.

Meditation: Scripture everywhere recognizes the living power of a great example (7).

Hebrews 13.17-25

As he comes to the close of his letter our author has some final advice for his readers. He begins with a further reference to the place of Christian leaders. All too often church members are harshly critical of their pastors and other ministers, and their attitude may do harm to the cause of Christ. We should not, of course, suggest that ministers are above criticism. They are imperfect men and just as liable as anybody else to make mistakes. But they have important work to do and it will be hindered and not helped if they are the objects of constant attacks and criticism. Moreover, typically, they are men who have a deep concern for the wellbeing of their people. They 'are keeping watch over your souls, as men who will have to give account' (17). It is well, accordingly, that those who are committed to their care so act that these leaders can render their account 'joyfully, and not sadly'. Even if a church member disagrees with his leaders it is of no advantage to him if they have to render a sad account of him (17).

These same leaders are always in need of the help their followers can give by their prayers. So is the writer of the Epistle, and he puts in his personal request for his friends to help him by their intercessions (18 f.). This leads him into a magnificent benediction which has been a help to Christians throughout the centuries. It characterizes God as 'the God of peace' and reminds us of His part in bringing about the resurrection of our Lord. Our Lord's care for us comes out in the description of Him as 'the great Shepherd of the sheep'. Then we revert to the thought of God's constancy. He has done all this 'by the blood of the eternal covenant', i.e. the blood that Christ shed is the means of bringing about a covenant which will never be replaced. Since the Son of God Himself mediated this covenant it is final. Then we come back to the thought of what God will do in His people, equipping them for service, and the benediction is rounded off with an ascription of glory for ever. There are some personal notes, one of which speaks warmly of Timothy (23), and the Epistle is completed with 'the grace'.

Thought: If He became our High Priest by laying down His life, what can He not do with what we lay down?

Questions for further discussion and meditation on Hebrews 12,13

1. In what ways is Christ our example?
2. Relate the teaching of ch. 12 on discipline as a mark of sonship to your own circumstances.
3. Discuss the hindrances modern life presents to attaining that 'holiness without which no one will see the Lord' (12.14). How can they be overcome?
4. What conditions must we fulfil if we are to offer to God 'acceptable worship' (12.28)?
5. How far are the directions of ch. 13 applicable to modern life?

James

Not a great deal can be said about this little writing. Its original readers are quite unknown. It is in the form of a letter, but it is not certain whether it should be taken as a real letter meant for a certain definite circle of recipients. There are no personal details such as would be expected in a writing of that sort, and the address is general. It reads much like a sermon, a little exhortation to fulfil the duties of Christian men, and to remember the essence of Christian teaching.

And if nothing definite is known of the original readers the same must be said of the author. He tells us that his name is James, and he describes himself only as 'a servant of God and of the Lord Jesus Christ', a description that would fit all of God's servants. As James was a fairly common name among the early Christians this makes it difficult for us to be precise in our ascription of authorship. It is often held that the James in question was James the Lord's brother, and that he is identical with the James who is so prominent in *Acts*. This may well be so, and it would explain the authoritative tone in which the letter is written. But it must be recognized that there is a good deal that is speculative here. In the end our verdict will probably have to be that we do not know for certain who wrote the letter, though James the Lord's brother is a possibility.

Just as there is uncertainty as to writer and readers, so there is doubt as to the date of the writing. Nothing dates it with any exactness and we are not likely to get beyond the position that it is undoubtedly early. No advanced stage of ecclesiastical development seems indicated, and the section on faith and works looks early. After Paul's writings had become widely accepted it is not easy to see a writer producing something which might be construed as opposing the great Apostle.

But if there are many uncertainties one thing is plain—we would be greatly impoverished without this little writing. Zahn speaks of the author as 'a preacher who speaks like a prophet . . . in language which for forcibleness is without parallel in early Christian literature, excepting the discourses of Jesus.' Moffatt cites this and goes on to point out that in 108 verses there are no less than 54 imperatives. This is a forthright writing stressing the importance of practical Christian action.

James is content to see himself as occupying a very lowly place, for he speaks of himself as a servant (or slave) of God. Notice that he links God and 'the Lord Jesus Christ'. He had come to see Jesus as occupying the very highest place of all. He addresses his Epistle to 'the twelve tribes in the Dispersion', which raises more than one problem. There do not appear to have been twelve tribes in existence at the time, or if there were, they were not in evidence. Again, the 'Dispersion' was a technical term for the Jews dispersed throughout the ancient world, the Jews outside Palestine, but it seems very unlikely that James was writing to the Jews as such. It thus seems likely that we should take 'the twelve tribes' as a reference to Israel indeed, but the spiritual Israel, the Church regarded as the people of God. The reference to the Dispersion will then indicate that it is the Church at large, the Church throughout the world, that is in mind and not Christians in any specific area.

To Christians at large, then, James writes on the necessity for constancy. We do not like difficulties and trials. We regard them as unfortunate necessities to be borne with as good a grace as possible. James sees them as occasions for joy (2). His point is that it is only through trials that we are able to develop the quality of steadfastness. The N.T. has a number of such exhortations to remind us that in the piping days of peace we do not really develop spiritual fibre. That comes about rather in the process of grappling with difficulties. Trials are not pleasant but the Christian should never face them in the same spirit as does the non-Christian. For the Christian, suffering has been transformed by the suffering of Christ. It is seen now as the means through which God can bring about great good. It is accordingly not to be regarded as an occasion for rebellion, but of progress in the faith. So, too, the Christian must be constant in the face of lack of wisdom and of doubt. He can look to God for all that is needed, knowing that nothing needful will be held back. But the blessing is not for the double-minded (7 f.). Steadfastness is a necessity if we are to go forward in the Christian life.

Thought: If you are wise you will ask for wisdom.

James 1.9-18   God's Good Gifts

We are always tempted to use a wrong set of values. It is natural for men to think of wealth as of great importance, and indeed there are few among mankind who do not make a serious effort to acquire a generous slice of this world's goods. James reminds us that riches will fail (11), and he goes so far as to say that it is 'the lowly brother' who should 'boast in his exaltation' (9). When a poor man receives the gospel he becomes rich in the things that really matter. He is exalted, and, though he lacks earthly wealth, he may well rejoice. Likewise the rich man who becomes a Christian has matter for rejoicing, but this time in his 'humiliation'. Like the poor man's exaltation this will refer to a spiritual condition. It is not that the rich man loses any of his wealth (though it is quite possible that his becoming a Christian will mean the loss of certain sources of gain). Rather, he has learned the true place of riches (and the place of true riches) and no longer thinks of himself in the same way. He has learned real lowliness.

A similar lesson lies behind James' next section (12-15). He counsels his readers to regard times of testing in the right way. It is a blessed thing, not a disaster, to undergo testing. The man who enjoys this experience is also learning a sense of values. To survive testing is the way to 'the crown of life' (12). This includes an understanding of the meaning of temptation, namely, that it does not come from God, but from a man's own desire. And the end result of giving way to it is death (15).

Thus both poverty and a right attitude to wealth are gifts of God. So, too, in another way, are trials. God never sends temptations, but He uses them for the upbuilding of His people. So James goes on to notice that every good gift really comes from God. Our attention may be fixed on some intermediary through whom the gift comes. But it is God who is the author. And He is not subject to change. Thus whether what comes to us seems pleasant or the reverse we can take it as from the hand of a God who never ceases to give good gifts to His children.

James 1.19-27   Deeds, not Words

Most of us like to hear ourselves talking, and in any conversation enjoy getting our view point across. And most of us like to be sure that our own interests are properly safeguarded. We all too easily become angry when we are thwarted. James reminds us that both attitudes can imperil our spiritual development. It is a much sounder policy to listen first. The Christian should be slow both to speech and to anger (19). He should make the effort to put away all evil decisively and to receive that word from God which brings salvation (21). In view of the way some have misinterpreted this Epistle, as though it were giving expression to a doctrine of salvation by works, it is well to notice this clear expression of the truth that salvation comes from 'the implanted word', not from anything that men do.

But this does not mean that our manner of life is unimportant. James is always ready to remind his readers of the importance of living out their faith. Now he uses the illustration of a man looking in a mirror, a casual glance which means very little. The man looks into the mirror and goes on his way forgetting even what it was he saw. Not in this light-hearted way should a man face his Christian obligations. For that, perseverance in well-doing is needed.

To show us the kind of thing he has in mind James turns attention to contrasting religions (26 f.). That which is not characterized by control of the tongue (cf. v. 19) is 'vain', i.e. empty. There is nothing in it. The man is self-deceived. Real religion, by contrast, comes out in a man's attitude to the defenceless. The orphans and widows were proverbial in the ancient world for poverty and defencelessness. They had no man to act as their protector and were easy prey for the unscrupulous. They normally found it very difficult to earn their living and had little redress if exploited. So it is a mark of a genuine religion to look out for such in their affliction and help them. They could make no return.

James 2.1-7   The Rich and the Poor

Clearly the problem of the right attitude to rich men exercised James greatly. Paul tells us that there were not many men of family and position in the Corinthian church (1 Cor. 1.26 ff.), and this would no doubt have been true fairly universally. There is no reason for doubting that the first converts to Christianity came largely from the depressed classes. They were poor men, or even slaves. According to the accepted standards of their day, they had been used to giving deference to the wealthy and the well placed. When they became Christians they quite naturally carried the attitude over into their new life. This natural human tendency must have been strengthened by the equally natural human tendency to be very solicitous of the few rich men who were converted. They would tend to be highly esteemed in the little Christian assemblies and to be given especial consideration, even deference.

This kind of treatment is not easy to reconcile with a proper Christian understanding of life. If all men are sinners, and all stand in need of divine salvation, then no man, no matter how wealthy, is anything other than a suppliant for the divine mercy. James reminds his readers that the kind of conduct which singles out the rich for special consideration is contrary to important Christian teachings. It means that the men who do this have set themselves up as judges, as they make distinctions between one believer and another, and, moreover, 'judges with evil thoughts' (4).

It is also the case that the poor more commonly than the rich are 'rich in faith' (5). This does not mean that God rejects the rich. Rather it arises from the fact that all too often those who have great material possessions give way to the temptation to put their trust in them. They cut themselves off from humble, dependent faith. James adds one practical point. It was the rich and not the poor who were usually responsible for the oppression which overtook the Christians from time to time. As a class it was the rich rather than the poor who blasphemed the name of God by their conduct (7). In an affluent society such warnings are very much in point.

James 2.8-13 The Royal Law

It might have been objected that James was making too much of this one point. After all, it is a natural tendency, and it is only a small thing. James' reply is twofold: in the first place it is not a small thing, and in the second it is a sin and all sin is serious.

It is not a small thing, for the supremely important thing in living the Christian life is to practise love. James calls the injunction, 'You shall love your neighbour as yourself', the 'royal law'. That is to say, it is the supreme law, that law which matters above all others. It accords with the words of our Lord Himself when He summed up the obligations resting on His followers to love both God and man (Mark 12.29-31). It is not without its interest that the command to love one's neighbour as oneself is taken from Lev. 19.18, and that in the immediate context we read, 'you shall not be partial to the poor or defer to the great' (Lev. 19.15). Thus to give special consideration to the rich, while putting the poor in a place of low esteem, means to go contrary to what is laid down in the law of God. It is to commit sin. Those who do this are transgressors (9).

Nor is there a defence that it is only a minor commandment that has been broken. To break any commandment is to become a law-breaker. This is often lost sight of. Almost everybody in our society thinks he is living, on the whole, a fairly good life (it is the other people who do the really bad things). He is usually ready to admit that there are some things he does which he ought not and that there are some things he does not do which he should. But it always seems to work out that the really serious sins are never those he commits. In the face of this very common and very natural human attitude James still has something to say. To break a law of God, any law, is to become a law-breaker. Nobody who thinks seriously about it can regard any sin as unimportant. We are responsible people. One day we must give account of ourselves to God. Judgement is a serious business. But James' last word is on mercy (13).

James 2.14-26   Faith and Works

Nowhere does James' strong emphasis on practical Christianity come out more clearly than here. Indeed, so prominent is it that some have felt that James is contradicting Paul. Paul, they say, teaches that a man is justified by faith, not works (Gal. 2.16), whereas here James is teaching the opposite and indeed goes so far as to say that 'a man is justified by works and not by faith alone' (24).

It is important not to be hypnotized by words, but to ask what James means. And it is quite plain when we try to answer this question that James does not mean by works what Paul means. Paul is speaking of those works done in obedience to the law whereby a man tries to merit his salvation. Unweariedly Paul combats this error. Men cannot acquire their salvation by works of law. But James is not talking about this at all when he looks for works. The works of which he speaks are the outworking of a living faith. Indeed he says specifically, 'I by my works will show you my faith' (18). Works are the evidence that faith is present. For James faith is undoubtedly important (see 1.6; 2.1,5; 5.15). He assumes that faith is necessary. But he denies that a right faith can exist without works. The kind of faith that lacks works is dead (17).

The faith James has in mind in this section of the Epistle is something very different indeed from what Paul means by faith (or for that matter what James means elsewhere). We are not left to guess at this, for he tells us plainly what this kind of faith is like: 'You believe that God is one; you do well. Even the demons believe—and shudder' (19). This is not the warm personal trust in a living Saviour which is what Paul means by faith. James then is opposing something which Paul is not advocating. There is no contradiction.

Finally, let us notice that James' point is important. It is always easier to make a profession of faith than it is to make good that profession in a life lived in the service of God. But it is that to which we are called. James calls attention to Abraham and Rahab as people who lived out their faith. Saving faith is a faith that works by love (as Paul puts it, Gal. 5.6).

Questions for further study and discussion on James 1,2

1. What may we learn from this part of James about constancy?
2. How is James' emphasis on an active faith relevant to your situation?
3. Discuss James' treatment of riches and poverty.
4. How does James bring out the seriousness of sin?
5. What tendencies do you discern in the modern church toward the kind of error that James opposes in 2.14–26?

James 3.1-5   Teachers and the Judgement

It appears from the opening verse that there was a tendency in some parts of the Church to seek the teaching office. Some men always find the limelight attractive, and there were not many opportunities for finding it in the early Church. Christians seem to have been fairly closely knit as a band of brothers in Christ. There was not much opportunity for showing off before others. But teaching did put a man in a position of prominence, and men of a certain temperament sought the position in consequence. While a man should not avoid any responsibility that God lays upon him, he should not seek a post of which this could not be said. So James begins by pointing out that those who teach will be judged very strictly. It is still a principle to be carefully observed that greater privilege means greater responsibility.

The danger involved in this is that men are apt to make mistakes (2), and more particularly in the things they say. A slip of the tongue with serious consequences is always a possibility. And it is more of a possibility for the teacher than for other people. Words are his tools of trade. He uses them of necessity to convey his meaning. So to rush into a position of teaching means to thrust oneself into a situation where a dangerous error is an ever-present possibility.

This leads James to the reflection that the tongue, though small in size, is great in achievement. He finds three illustrations of this: the small bit that guides a large horse, the small rudder that steers a huge ship, and the little fire that kindles a whole forest. We should not be misled by the tongue's small size. Small though it is, it is powerful. It is the tongue that enables the teacher or the preacher to make his point. It is by the tongue that the ordinary Christian can witness to others and so win them for Christ. So James' warning on the responsibility of using aright a weapon with great potential is of wider application than simply to teachers.

Having shown that the tongue is able to accomplish great results and should not be underestimated because of its small size James goes on to the further point that it is fraught with great possibilities for evil as well as for good. Rightly used, our words accomplish much in the service of God. Wrongly used they bring about incalculable damage. In a vigorous verse James speaks of the tongue as 'an unrighteous world' (which indicates the extent of its influence as well as its bias toward evil), as 'staining the whole body' (I am wholly defiled when I misuse my tongue; it is not only a part of me that is affected), and as setting on fire the whole of 'the round circle of existence' (Moffatt). This last expression is a very unusual one, but Moffatt probably gives us the sense of it. James is carrying on the metaphor of the forest fire and indicating that the tongue can start an evil which will spread throughout the world. And its origin? It is 'set on fire by hell'. There is something satanic about the wrong use of the tongue.

James further notes that man has shown great skill as a tamer of beasts, and he uses this as yet another way of bringing out the evil caused by wrong speech. In strong contrast with his ability to handle the wildest of beasts is man's inability to control his tongue. James speaks of it as 'a restless evil, full of deadly poison', the last expression being probably suggested by his reference to reptiles (7). The poisonous tongues of snakes are often referred to in antiquity.

James' final point under this heading is that this is all unnatural. It is incongruous to use the same mouth for blessing as cursing. This is quite contrary to what we see in nature, for example in springs where the water is either fresh or brackish but not both, or in trees where the fruit is consistent. The moral is obvious. It is clear to all God's servants that they should bless and praise Him. All their other speech should be consistent with this. This sets the tone for their words to men.

Thought: 'Silence may be a sign of sanctification' (G. Scroggie).

James 3.13-18 True Wisdom

From the tongue James moves to the life as a whole and he contrasts the wise man with the unwise, though he does not use the latter term. Rather he speaks of a 'wisdom' not of heavenly origin. Just as earlier he has spoken of every good gift as coming from God (1.17), so now he thinks of all true wisdom as 'from above'. The main point which concerns him is the self-assertion of the wicked, which he finds in sharp contrast to the meekness of God's own.

Meekness, incidentally, was not universally regarded as a virtue in the Greek world. It was held that a real man would stand up for his rights and not allow himself to be trampled on. It was humiliating not to be accorded one's full rights and one's proper place. Rivals must not be allowed to usurp one's proper privileges and the like. Thus what James is castigating as 'bitter jealousy and selfish ambition' (14) was usually regarded as a proper concern for one's rightful position. The point, and it is important, is that the Christian does not take his standards from the world.

There is a reversal of values when a man knows himself to have been saved by Christ. He himself can contribute nothing to the process. His sins have been put away not by his own best effort, but by Christ's atoning death. He sees that he has sinned against God, but that God has refused to damn him. Instead, in the person of His Son, He has suffered to save him. When the significance of this has sunk in, a man cannot be selfish and self-assertive. In his measure he reacts to others as God has acted towards him, that is, in forgiving love. So he looks for that wisdom which is from above. He looks now for purity in his own life, and for an attitude of peaceableness and mercy to other men (17). He rejects jealousy and ambition as devilish (15). The connection between righteousness and peace (18) is noteworthy. The world has not yet realized, in its deep yearning for peace, that peace and righteousness are intimately connected. It is still not possible to have real peace if in our self-seeking we reject real righteousness.

James 4.1-4 The Cause of War

It is possible that James is not speaking in the first instance about wars in the military sense. He may well be using military imagery to castigate quarrels among church members. But what he says has relevance to a wider circle than quarrelsome Christians. To an age as eager for peace and as much given to war as ours these words about the root causes of wars come home with force and relevance. For the fact is that if we promote a warlike spirit it is only to be expected that we will have wars, and this whether on the grand scale between nations or on the small scale between church members. We must get down to the basic issues.

James is stressing the extremely important point that the cause of hostility is basically human passion. Men desire. Men covet. And their passions are so strong that they take into their own hands the gratification of their desires. This is the spirit that leads nations to wars and individuals to quarrels. Wherever men or nations act on the assumption that they themselves are the guardians of their own rights and that they are quite entitled to take whatever steps they deem necessary to safeguard those rights, then enmity is inevitable. For the attitude is certain to be met by a similar attitude on the side of the other party. So hostility results and this may well result in open warfare on a grand or minor scale.

For the Christian there is a further reflection that the reason he does not have what he needs is that he does not ask (2). Prayer is a mighty force. And when some of his readers are prepared to retort that they *have* prayed, James replies that they have prayed wrongly. They have tried to use prayer for the gratification of those same passions! Instead of renouncing the worldly way, they have thought they could enlist God on their side. Even in what they take to be a proper religious activity they have been manifesting a worldly spirit. They (and we) must learn that the world's friendship means enmity with God (4). There is a fundamental incompatibility here, and as long as we gloss over it with words, while retaining the worldly spirit of self-aggrandizement, we must expect strife.

James 4.5-10   God's Yearning

In rejecting the way of the world James does not want it thought that he is advocating in God's name a course which would mean anything less than the very best for God's people. God calls on men to reject the way of self-aggrandizement, but not because He wants to cramp them into a narrow and unsatisfying existence. Rather, the reverse is the case. In bold anthropomorphic language James pictures God as yearning jealously over us, as longing for us so that He may bring us into that perfect fellowship with Him, which is our best good. The exact source of the quotation in v. 5 is not clear. It seems to be a free and somewhat poetic rendering of the thought of Exod. 20.5. And its exact meaning is not plain either. The RSV takes 'spirit' to mean the human spirit over which God yearns. But it might refer to the Holy Spirit with the meaning, 'the Spirit which dwells within us yearns jealously over us'. Either way the thought is that God longs for us to find our rest in Him.

Quite in this spirit He gives us grace (6), a thought which accords with Prov. 3.34, for the proud do not look for God's grace, whereas the humble gratefully accept it. James launches into a series of exhortations, the burden of which is 'Follow the right way, and you will certainly receive the blessing of God'. James is making with some emphasis the point that God is always ready to give His blessing, but that it is quite possible for men to adopt a self-seeking way of life that cuts them off from God's help. So we should resist the devil, not yield to him (7). We should submit to God (7), and draw near to Him (8), when we will find that He will draw near to us. But our attitude must be wholehearted. This means a thoroughgoing purification (8) and a genuine sorrow for sin (9). But the man who really humbles himself before God will surely find that God will not abandon him. God will exalt him (10).

James 4.11-17   The Will of God

One of the commonest human frailties is that of setting oneself up over the law. Often it is in a comparatively minor matter, as when Christian motorists determine their own speed limits instead of abiding by those laid down by authority. Sometimes it is in a matter of great importance and the climax is reached with the criminal who defies all authority and acts according to his own desires and his conception of his own profit. A proper regard for the law is a necessity if men are to live in community. James is concerned, however, not simply with community life but with the attitude of the Christian to law. He is concerned at the way Christians sometimes act as though they are superior to law. The particular manifestation of it with which he deals is that of speaking evil of others. Gossip and slander are more than the social pastime they appear to be. They proceed from an attitude of mind which presumes to sit in judgement on others, and which is thus arrogating to itself a function that belongs to God alone. This is a dangerous practice as well as a wicked one, for the God whose place the slanderer usurps is One who is able to destroy as well as to save (12). None of us is so great (or so safe!) that he can engage in criticism of his fellow servants.

Men sometimes ignore the will of God in other matters, as when they plan without taking God into account. James does not mean that we should not exercise reasonable forethought in planning our affairs. That is only a correct use of our God-given intelligence. He is opposing the attitude whereby a Christian plans as though he were a worldly man, completely ignoring God. All our plans should include 'If the Lord wills', a provision which is not met by making up our minds and simply adding D.V.

The final verse in this chapter is notable. We usually think of sins of commission as the important ones and tend to overlook altogether the good we might have done. James reminds us that it is important to make use of every opportunity of doing good.

Failure to do good is not simply a matter for mild regret. It is sin.

Question: Link the principle in v. 17 with that in Rom. 14.23; do these represent a complete rule of conduct for the believer?

James 5.1-6 The Perils of Riches

It is clear that in the church with which James was concerned there were problems posed by the activities of the wealthy. He has had occasion earlier in the Epistle to rebuke a wrong use of riches. As he returns to the theme we should not think that this is an obsession with something that does not matter or does not matter greatly. Through all the centuries of the Church's existence it has been the case that many whose faith stood firm in the days of doubt and difficulty have not been able to withstand affluence. The Christian life is always a battle and to the poor this is very plain. But for the rich some of the struggle has been taken out of life and it is easy for them to lose their grip on spiritual realities. The possession of a degree of affluence all too often leads to a strong desire for greater affluence and so to that love of money which is the root of every kind of evil (1 Tim. 6.10).

James clearly has in mind at this point some rich men who had engaged in oppressing the poor. He is not talking about riches in general, but about men known to him and his readers who had defrauded their labourers (4). This is a good example of the kind of temptation to which the rich are exposed and which does not confront the poor to anything like the same degree. The rich in their desire to be richer may press on without regard to the rights of others. When this happens their riches may be said to have 'rotted' and the like (2 f.). Incidentally, when James speaks of gold and silver as having 'rusted' (3) this should not be taken as evidence of ignorance of the properties of precious metals. James is not speaking of physical and chemical properties. He is referring to the fact that wealth obtained by improper means is not ultimately lasting. The rich, like all men, will stand before God's judgement, and their riches will then be found of no avail. There may also be the thought that these riches are tarnished. James is giving a serious and very vigorous warning. No man can use his wealth to the detriment of others and expect to get away with it when he stands before God. An affluent generation does well to heed the warning.

Thought: 'It is better to be oppressed than an oppressor' (G. Scroggie).

There are two Greek words which are sometimes translated 'patience', and we have both of them in this passage. The one means very much what we mean by patience. It contains the idea of longsuffering. It is formed on exactly the model of a word which means 'short-tempered' and is its opposite, i.e. 'long-tempered'. It is a refusal to give way to provocation. It is a readiness to put up with contradiction and baseless opposition. It is a steady refusal to lose one's temper in the face of frustration. There is nothing that one can do about this kind of opposition except be provoked by it or endure it. It is this that James has in mind when he speaks of the farmer. There is nothing he can do about the weather, or the seasons. When he has planted his crop he must wait patiently. But in his patient waiting he knows that the time of harvest is surely coming. And the Christian knows that the time of this world's harvest is coming. He must endure innumerable provocations and frustrations. But he can bear them all with patience, for he knows that his Lord will one day come. The last word is not with those who provoke and frustrate. The last word is with the Lord. Since His coming is sure we may settle our hearts (8).

The other word means steadfastness rather than patience. It is the attitude of the soldier who in the midst of the hardest battle is not dismayed by the hard knocks he receives but lays about him with a right good will. There is an air of activity, even aggressiveness, about it. James uses this word of Job (11). That patriarch came through triumphant. While perhaps James does not want us to differentiate too sharply between his two words they do have different emphases and we can profit by reflecting on both. James' final statement in v. 11 should be borne in mind in all troubles. The Lord who permits them is compassionate and merciful.

Verse 12 reminds us that our word should be reliable always. James is not concerned with the problem of oaths in law courts and the like. He is saying that in ordinary life our word should not need to be bolstered by an oath before it can be accepted.

James 5.13-20   The Prayer of Faith

Throughout this Epistle we have seen that James is strongly practical. He is greatly concerned with the way Christians live out their faith. Now in his concluding section he gives attention to prayer, possibly the most powerful weapon in the Christian's armoury, and certainly a potent factor in the everyday life of the believer. He relates prayer to suffering and to sickness. In the latter case he suggests that the elders of the church should pray over the sick man and anoint him with oil in the Lord's name (14). Many have pointed out that in heathen religions there was widespread use of incantations and the like in times of sickness, and the thought is that James is advocating a Christian practice that would replace this kind of thing. Be that as it may, his emphasis is not on the oil but on prayer. It is 'the prayer of faith' that 'will save the sick man' (15). James also sees this as connected with the man's spiritual condition. Forgiveness of sins is to be sought and will be granted. This is the point also of the mutual confession advocated in v. 16. It is not a sacramental confession but a mutual sharing of grief, with prayer for healing. Christians should be concerned about one author's spiritual condition and be constant in prayer for each other. James goes on to cite Elijah as a well-known example of the power of prayer. That power, which caused first drought and then rain, he feels, is very applicable to believers.

This brings him on to his final topic, that of soul-winning. To bring men back from sin to Christ is to bring them into salvation. It will cover all their sins. Nothing could be more worthwhile.

In all our concern for sickness and sinners we should not overlook the fact that James has something for those whose souls are in health (13). The cheerful should sing praise. It is God who is the source of all their blessings and it is well that they recognize it.

Questions for further study and discussion on James 3–5
1. What are your own sins of the tongue? How can you guard against them?
2. What is the relevance for our generation of James' words about war?
3. Apply James' teaching on doing the will of God to your own situation.
4. In what circumstances in modern life may we apply the teachings of James about patience and endurance?
5. Discuss the relation between prayer and the cure of sickness.